POTATO CHIPS ARE VEGETABLES

Also by Carole Achterhof

NEVER TRUST A SIZE THREE

POTATO CHIPS ARE VEGETABLES

Written and Illustrated by

CAROLE ACHTERHOF

Cover design by KEITH VAN WESTEN

Bare Bones Books
Luverne, MN 56156

Dedicated to my daughters,
Kristin, Linda and Marta

Bare Bones Books
315 North Freeman
Luverne, MN 56156

Distributed by
Prairie House, Inc.
Suite F
1335 Second Avenue North
Fargo, ND 58201

Library of Congress Catalog Card Number: 91-76686
ISBN 0-9625940-1-6

Printed in the United States by
Crescent Publishing, Inc., Hills, MN 56138

First Printing

Table of Contents

Potato Chips are Vegetables

As if it wasn't bad enough to have medical professionals telling us how bad junk food is for our health, California legislators have now added the final insult.

They have created a new "snack tax". By the way, "snack tax" is impossible to say three times in rapid succession with a mouthful of potato chips.

Although the new tax is expected to add $200 million dollars to the state budget, legislators are having a tough time determining which items constitute "snack foods".

So far, chocolate chips aren't taxed, but chocolate kisses are. Cupcakes are taxable, but doughnuts aren't. Shoppers and store owners are absolutely confused.

I may have a solution for them. It's a system I've devised over the years to separate "good food" (your basic food groups) from "junk food".

For example, all foods with the names of vegetables are essential for a well-balanced diet and shouldn't be taxed. These foods include caramel corn, corn chips, potato chips and potato sticks.

The same holds true for foods with the names of dairy products. This group would include cheese curls, cream-filled eclairs and cupcakes, buttermints and anything containing milk chocolate.

In the same way that foods with one syllable are accepted universally as being good for us (meat, beans, bread, milk), any other food with one syllable should be equally accepted. Taxes shouldn't be placed on monosyllabic fudge, tortes, pies or cakes.

However, moderation should be exercised with all of these foods. They should not be eaten while you're still standing at the checkout counter, but quaffing them down in the parking lot is perfectly acceptable.

Speaking of moderate behavior, it's also a good idea to remove the wrappers before enjoying any of these foods. It may cause a slight delay, but you will gain the respect of those around you.

California legislators opened up a whole new can of "gummy worms" when they decided to tax snack foods. They should have applied the taxes to lima beans, liver and other vital organs from animals.

Those taxes might not have yielded $200 million, but a buck's a buck.

My Life as a Negative Stripper

It sounded like an interesting job.

I've heard the statistics about the average person making three career changes in a lifetime, but after living a dual-career as Lois Lane and Our Miss Brooks, I didn't think about a third possibility.

The ad in the weekly newspaper read, "Wanted: NEGATIVE STRIPPER. Minimum four years experience. Immediate opening in a growing, well established company. Call Bob." The ad also gave a phone number.

I've never given much thought to going public as a stripper with a bad attitude, but I certainly have the background.

My first experience in negative stripping took place in September, 1954, when I began seventh grade and my phy ed class was taught by an overzealous woman who was obviously obsessed with shower checks. Her demands that we lather up after every gym class made me suspect that she was receiving kickbacks from a soap company.

Stripping down to the buff in the company of 30 more-endowed classmates was unsettling, to say the least. My only solution was to shroud myself in the skimpy school-issued towels and to remain inconspicuous.

The towel-in-the-shower ruse worked really well until the day I slipped on a bar of soap as I entered the shower room. My negative attitude can be traced back to that fateful day when my towel flew east and the rest of me headed west.

My bad attitude worsened in later years when I was required to undress for medical checkups. Although people always say that a body is no more to someone in the medical profession than a car is to a mechanic, I still feel strange about taking off my clothes in an office building.

It seems to get worse as my mileage increases.

If being a negative stripper means disrobing and saying things like "So, what's it to ya?" and "You want me to take off WHAT?", I'm the woman for the job.

Out of curiosity, I called the number in the ad. A very nice woman answered the phone and told me that a negative stripper works in a camera room. There was also something in the job description about shooting negatives and preparing them for plates. It was all very technical.

While the phone call was informative, it became clear that what the company wanted and what I had to offer were two different things.

The job wasn't perfect, after all.

Putting on the Squeeze

The Tube Council of North America is upset.

Few of us bothered to observe the recent 150th anniversary of the squeezable tube, evidently a big deal to people in the tube industry.

In light of the trouble that the squeezable tube has caused in most homes, they should feel fortunate the anniversary slipped by unnoticed.

There is finally someone to blame for the squabbles arising from finding a toothpaste tube squeezed in the middle or left uncapped on the shelf. According to the council, the patent for the squeezable tube was filed on September 11, 1841, by a landscape painter, John Goffe Rand.

While trying to think of a way to carry his paints outside, he came up with the bright idea of soldering pieces of lead together, forming tubes. Toothpaste wasn't packaged in tubes until 50 years later.

You don't have to be a mathematician to figure out that toothpaste tubes have been creating discord in families for 100 years.

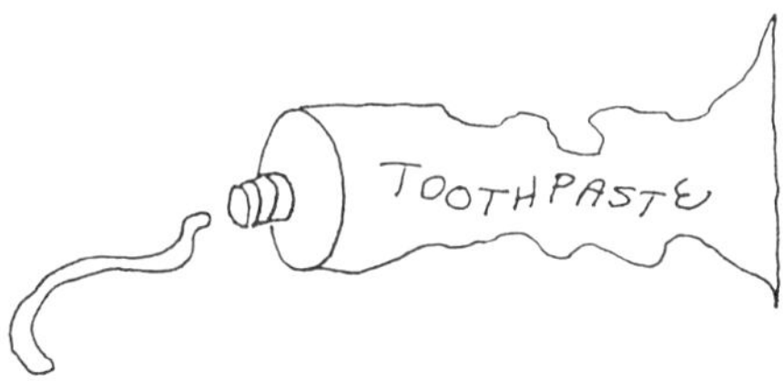

When it comes to toothpaste tubes, ours is a mixed marriage.

I descended from a long line of tube squeezers. The act of squeezing a tube in its middle is a simple act of aggressive behavior, with the tube representing the necks of employers, siblings or parents. It is also a pleasurable experience, not unlike taking an Oreo apart and eating the frosting first or getting the first whiff of a newly opened can of ground coffee.

There was a disadvantage to squeezing a

toothpaste tube in the middle, particularly before the invention of plastic tubes. Invariably, the tube's sides would split open and toothpaste would be smeared over every surface in the bathroom.

While I was growing up, bothersome tube caps were considered to be one-use items.

My husband's upbringing was much more organized. Like half of the country's population, he's a firm believer in meticulously rolling toothpaste tubes up from their bottoms and painstakingly extracting every iota of toothpaste from a tube. He would no more leave a toothpaste tube uncapped than he would leave the house undressed.

There's a certain element of suspense with an uncapped tube of toothpaste. If the tube has been sitting out long enough for the exposed toothpaste to harden to the consistency of sidewalk cement, there's excitement in squeezing the tube and waiting for the explosion of toothpaste when the dried gunk is released.

It's the same excitement as trying to shake thick catsup out of a thin-necked bottle. While shaking the upside-down bottle for countless times, a person can never be sure when the catsup will finally spew forth like a volcanic eruption.

If not for John Goffe Rand, my life wouldn't be nearly as exciting as it is. Neither would our marriage.

"Judge Not"

Words can come back to haunt us.

As I watched the television coverage of Clarence Thomas before the Senate Judiciary Committee, that truth was especially evident. Every speech he had every given and every opinion he had ever written were given the fine-comb treatment.

Although I agree with the process of appointing a person to the highest court in the land, I doubt whether many of us could survive similar scrutiny. Some words are best left forgotten.

After considerable soul-searching - a task requiring four or five minutes - I've come up with a list of statements I wish I'd never made.

1945 - " When I grow up, I'm going to be just like my mother."

1962 - "Of course, I'll marry you. All I want in life is to cook three meals for you everyday, to iron your shirts and to have your children."

1963 - "Why would we need a color television? If we want to see a movie in color, we can see it at the movie theater."

1964 - "Golf is for people who have nothing better to do with their time."

1965 - "Is it over? Well, one thing's for certain. I'm never going to have another baby. I'll never go through that again. I'll never forget what it was like."

1966 - "Gosh, I miss having a little baby in the house. If I'm busy already, how much busier could I be with two or three more?"

1967 - "Let me out of this delivery room! I remember! I remember!"

1970 - "Once the kids are all in school, I'll get a job."

1971-1991 - "Well, I've done it. I've lost 40 pounds. I'll never gain that weight back again."

1984 - "I know it's rough leaving home and going off to college. But don't worry - I'll write every week."

1984 - "Once the kids are out of college, I'll quit working and cook meals for you again."

1987 - "Why would I ever want a word processor? All I need are my trusty electric typewriter and some correction fluid."

1989 - "Why should we buy a VCR? It's a waste of money. If we want to see a movie, we can always go to the movie theater."

1990 - "Let's plant lots of zucchini this spring."

1991 - "I never forget a name. As I was saying to what's-his-name last week, "At least we still have our memories."

Extra Padding

"Everything is for the best in this best of all possible worlds," wrote Voltaire.

The French writer and philosopher should have been around recently, when the world became even better for all of us pear-shaped women.

According to a group of Boston researchers, women with more padding on their back ends are less likely to suffer a hip fracture than women who are more slender. Only the researchers don't call it padding. They refer to it as "soft-tissue energy absorption capacity."

Remember - you read it here first. If you, too, are built like an Egyptian pyramid and your southern hemisphere is out of proportion, there's cause to celebrate.

Ever since I turned 40, and my cargo began to shift, I have been aware of the special advantages of carrying around a few extra pounds.

For one thing, there's little danger of freezing during the winter. Carrying extra padding on the body is not unlike insulating the walls and attic of a house. Body insulation is much easier and more fun to apply. I would choose chocolate over fiberglass anytime.

Those uncomfortable folding chairs at most committee meetings are also more bearable when a person is equipped with built-in cushions. If I only had a thin layer of epidermis between my bones and the chair seat, I doubt whether I would last much longer than the roll call. By gritting my teeth I might make it through the minutes of the last meeting.

The Boston research explains why only the gaunt faces of models are shown on the covers of fashion magazines. It would be bad for the fashion industry to show the models' body casts, clear evidence of their nasty falls.

Certain goals in my life have remained unobtainable: thin thighs, the Miss America title and willowy hips. Although I have accepted the fact that I will never hear Bert Parks sing "There she is..." and the Boston researchers have declared big hips to be a safety factor, only one hurdle remains.

If someone would come up with the health benefits of "thunder thighs", my life would be complete.

Learning French

I began my 44th first day of school last week. Like many returnees to the halls of learning, I worried about what to wear and whether I had enough school supplies. As I searched for my shoes (a nonessential item during the summer), I reminisced about those other first days.

One particular September stood out from all the rest as I prepared for another year in the classroom. That fall I was a freshman in college and it was the only time in my life I was asked to leave a class.

Although many teachers might have entertained the notion before I finally made it to college, Mademoiselle Meyer let me know in no uncertain terms that I was a persona non grata in French 101.

If not for the kissing incident, I would be a tri-linguist today. I could have been an interpreter at the United Nations. At least I would have impressed other customers at the grocery store with my ability to say "Where's the cream of chicken soup?" in three languages.

Memories of my encounter with the diminutive French teacher came back to me last week when I read about a new book, "Kissing: Everything You Ever Wanted to Know", by Tomina Edmark.

In her book, Edmark reveals some interesting facts about kissing. For example, Cleopatra is said not to have kissed any of her numerous lovers and the average U.S. female kisses 79 men before she marries.

Those facts alone lead me to two conclusions: Cleopatra's barge wasn't stocked with mouthwash and some women had more excitement than the rest of us.

If you can follow my logic, this all leads back to Mlle Meyer's French class.

After taking three years of high school Spanish, I hoped to pick up another language. In spite of my laissez faire approach to higher learning, the grimly determined Mlle Meyer expected us to become fluent in our new language during the first class session.

Our two views on education collided when I was told to repeat the phrase, "Et vous Monsieur Hughes?" As I was singled out to repeat the phrase over and over, I seriously questioned whether I would ever run up to a stranger and ask, "Are you Mr. Hughes?"

As soon as I would open my mouth, Mlle Meyer would shriek, "No! No! No!", which I soon figured out was the French equivalent of the English word, "No".

In desperation, she stood directly in front of me and slapped both of my cheeks with her hands.

"No! No! No!" she repeated. "You have no leep control!"

"I haven't had a date in two weeks," I offered apologetically. As the class broke up in nervous laughter, the bell sounded and the ordeal was over.

After class, Mlle Meyer took me aside and strongly suggested that I return to Spanish. I took her advice and studied Spanish for five more years.

This leads me to another conclusion about kissing: If you don't kiss, learning another language is next to impossible.

What's Russian for "Charge"?

I hate to rain on their parade, but the Russians have a long way to go before they can have a democracy like ours.

Government reorganization aside, specific changes will have to be made with their system of holidays and special days.

Without special holidays, stores would be unable to have sales, the backbone of our economic structure. Any country based on consumerism would face certain financial ruin it if didn't provide its citizens with good excuses to shop.

Our country wins hands down when it comes to setting days aside as holidays. Not only do we have commercial holidays like Easter, Thanksgiving, Christmas, New Year's Day and Valentine's Day, but we also have Mother's Day, Father's Day, Memorial Day, Labor Day and the Fourth of July. To fill in the gaps, and to keep us from going into shopping withdrawal, we observe January White Sale Days, Back-to-School Days, Secretaries' Day and Groundhog Day.

We are perhaps the only country with more holidays than there are days.

One of Russia's biggest problems with holidays will be determining which date will be their equivalent of our Fourth of July. According to the news accounts, August 22 (give or take a day) was when the country asserted its independence from the ruling communist party.

In terms of retail sales, another date should be seriously considered. August 22 simply doesn't cut it.

To illustrate this point, let's look at two independence days held in our neck of the woods: the

American "Fourth of July" and the Mexican "Cinco de Mayo".

To paraphrase Shakespeare, these dates "fall trippingly off the tongue." Fourth of July has four syllables; Cinco de Mayo has five.

Now consider "The Twenty-second of August", which has eight tongue-twisting syllables. The length alone would be an advertiser's nightmare. By the time the name of the holiday would be typeset, there would be room for little else in a newspaper ad.

It would also be cumbersome to say, "We're having a twenty-second of August picnic in our backyard, so bring your borscht."

The Russians already have a holiday on their calendar which would work rather well. The "Ninth of May", also known as Victory over Fascism Day, could be replaced with a celebration of this year's history-making events. A three-syllable date would have much more commercial value.

"Ninth of May Sale" would be a catchy slogan for shopping mall banners. As they say on Madison Avenue, let's run it up the flagpole and see who salutes.

Bad Advice

"Never give advice unless asked." - German proverb.

We're given all sorts of advice while we're young. Handed down from one generation to the next, some of the advice can warp our futures.

I've been giving considerable thought lately to the pearls of wisdom which were passed down to me while I was still in my formative years.

Mrs. Peterson, my fourth grade teacher, once told our class, "If you sleep on your left side, your heart may stop beating." It's only fair to mention that she uttered those words several years before the Russians launched Sputnik and some time after the invention of the wheel. Medical science was still in its infancy.

For at least six months, I lived in constant fear that I would roll to my left side during the night and wake up dead in the morning. There was no reason to doubt Mrs. Peterson. In my nine-year-old mind, teachers ranked right up there with angels and the President. Teachers were infallible.

I know now that I should have considered the source. When we would ask her why she was getting fatter by the week, she would giggle and say, "I don't know." She must have been surprised when she had a baby two weeks before the end of the school year.

She was also the teacher who promised, "Multiplication tables are easy." Her credibility wasn't all that stable.

One of my mother's favorite bits of advice was, "If you cross your eyes, they will stay that way." In order to drive the point home, she would often add, "I knew a girl who used to cross her eyes, and one day, they wouldn't move back."

My mother, a complex woman, could also combine advice and threats in one breath: "If you fall from that tree, you will kill yourself and don't come crying to me."

Later in life, I heard from at least a dozen sources, "If you carry your baby low, it's a boy." All of our babies were carried around the area of my knees, and they were all girls.

All of this advice came back to me when I read about a recent study done by field biologists engaged in a new area known as time budget analysis. They have discovered that the great majority of animals spend most of their time doing nothing constructive at all.

According to the biologists, expressions including "Busy as a beaver" and "Busy as a bee" are nothing more than myths. Even the industrious ant has been discredited. Outside of eating, courting and breeding, they do little else. They don't have work lists or schedules and they don't worry about stress management.

For years we have been told to emulate the animals' behavior. Bees, ants and beavers became the foundation of our national work ethic.

The biologists' research is good news for those of us who like to lie around doing very little during the "dog days" of August. Lying on our right sides, that is.

Say "Goodbye" and Pass the French Fries

We have become a drive-thru nation.

No longer content with driving up to impersonal windows for burgers and fries, we now have drive-thru divorces in Salem, OR, drive-thru weddings in Las Vegas, drive-thru pharmacies in Iowa and Indianapolis and drive-thru grocery shopping in California.

Be prepared now for the latest in "go-go" conveniences: drive-thru funeral parlors.

A funeral home in Nassawadoz, VA, now has a coffin-length window for people who wish to stay inside their cars while they bid a fond farewell to the dearly departed.

This truly is a mad, mad, mad, mad world.

I don't know about you, but when I'm finally displayed for all the world to see, I would rather not have the spectators munching on french fries and adjusting their car radios.

Many of us go to great lengths to look nice for that final public appearance. For what other reason do we diet, jog and exercise for most of our lives?

This may be a mobile socity, but drive-thru funeral homes seem to overstep the fine line of good taste.

Once accepted, it's very possible that the funeral homes will follow the trends already established by fast food restaurants.

"Hey, kids!" will blare the the TV commercials. "Be the first on your block to have a Grim Brothers Funeral Home fun-pack! For a limited time only, we will be offering pink plastic miniature caskets, perfect for your dolls, and bright yellow, plastic shovels, perfect for burying pet hamsters and gerbils in your backyard."

Coupons will be handed out for complimentary beverages and a few lucky customers will be singled out for sweepstakes prizes, including round-trip tickets to the Arlington National Cemetery.

Once the trend catches on, Morbid Mort, the funeral home clown, will be making guest appearances around the country with his trademark, a bouquet of black balloons.

Now that drive-thru funeral homes have become a reality, drive-thru baptisms, graduations and Bar Mitzvahs can't be far behind. Most of our social obligations will be met from the front seat of a car.

We will not longer have to struggle for the right words to say at a funeral or a wedding. There will no longer be a problem with deciding what to wear.

We will only have to honk as we drive by the window.

Avoid Furry Leftovers

While other people don't do windows, I don't do refrigerators.

Cleaning a refrigerator is an unsavory and somewhat dangerous activity. I question whether it's wise to have the possibly lethal contents of our refrigerator spread out on the kitchen table and every available counter for all the world to see.

To make matters worse, little plastic containers have to be pried open and sniffed to determine if the unidentifiable leftovers they hold are safe for human consumption.

If you've ever encountered a piece of pizza that has gone green or furry jello salad, you know what I'm talking about.

Cleaning out a refrigerator is definitely not for the faint-hearted or people who dislike surprises. That's why the manufacturers don't put windows on refrigerator doors.

What goes on behind a closed refrigerator door is definitely an example of "Out of sight, out of mind."

I personally choose not to interrupt the evolution of life forms on my refrigerator shelves. If microbes decide to marry, raise a family and sink into easy retirement somewhere between last Easter's ham and the leftover chili from last winter, I won't disturb their special moments.

In addition to my respect for lower life forms and

my reluctance to empty out an entire refrigerator, there is now another reason for leaving the appliance alone.

Gourmet ice is the latest trend to hit Japan and it's expected to arrive in the United States very soon. It's ice up to 10,000 years old that is chipped from Alaskan ice floes and is valued for its purity.

Although the ice cubes in my freezer aren't quite that old, it would be a shame to toss them out. Because my ice cubes have picked up the telltale scents of leftover bratwurst and spaghetti sauce they might not be considered to be true gourmet, but at least they don't have any stray mastadon hairs or pterodactyl droppings in them.

From now on, I will be quite the hit when it comes to entertaining guests.

"Would you like a drink? We have a very elegant treat for you this evening - ice cubes dating back to the Nixon era."

Very special guests could be offered freezer scrapings from the days of the Carter administration.

It's all a matter of looking at things differently. What may be ugly freezer buildup to one person may be gourmet ice to another.

Iowa Hunting Laws

Because of two new laws, which went into effect July 1, 1991, hunting in Iowa will never be the same.

The first law prohibits hunters from shooting across public highways. Although I'm surprised that no one thought of it before, it makes sense because we certainly don't want another Rushmore, MN.

Rushmore is a small town off Interstate 90 in southwestern Minnesota. Every summer, vacationing families from the East pull off into the tiny hamlet, expecting to see the gigantic stone faces of dead presidents.

When they are told that Mount Rushmore is another nine or ten hours to the west, they become horribly disoriented. In most cases, they crumple their roadmaps and burst into tears.

The same confusion would arise if Iowa hunters were allowed to shoot across public highways. Travelers, making their way from the East Coast to the West Coast, would assume they had reached the Los Angeles Freeway.

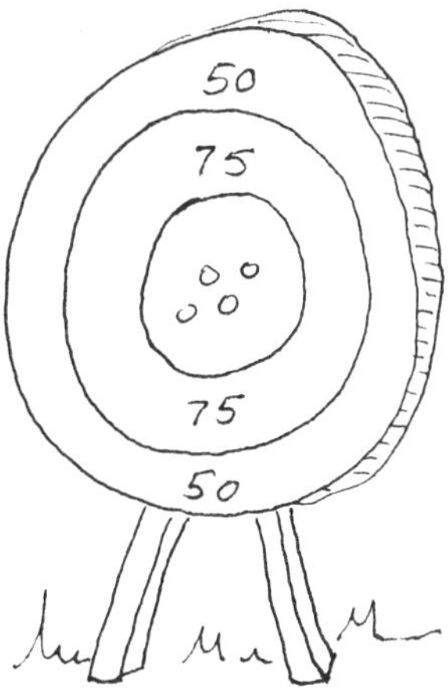

The second law makes it illegal to harass hunters. Why anyone would want to tease or taunt a person with a loaded gun, or for that matter, a loaded bow, is beyond me. I wonder what kind of insults were hurled before the law went into effect.

"Hey, fella! Nice pheasant. My grandmother's canary is bigger than that bird!"

"You know, with all of that camouflage clothing, you look like one big, walking forest. Have you considered wearing something a little less busy?"

"Nice shot. You missed the deer, but I think that tree's a goner."

"I've seen jackrabbits bigger than that deer!"

"Is that your deer on the truck hood? I'll bet Thumper and Flower are going to miss him."

The second law will no doubt make the rest of us kinder and gentler around hunters. I had respect for hunters long before the law was created. After all, they were wearing neon clothing long before it became fashionable.

I wonder why the law about hunter harassment was written. Did some state senator have a bad hunting experience? I also wonder if the punishment for hunter tormentors will be appropriate to the crime.

Will violators be required to reload endless cases of shotgun shells or will the hunter be allowed to turn on him in true Old West tradition?

If any hunter from Iowa has a logical explanation, I would like to hear it.

No offense intended.

Baby is Tutored

Until Baby joined our family three weeks ago, I knew very little about male cats.

To be honest, most of my knowledge about cats came from the television. I knew that Bob Barker wouldn't rest until every feline was spayed or neutered. After one particularly unsettling Alfred Hitchcock episode I learned that cats can break their owners' necks by tripping them as they walked downstairs. From watching TV commercials, I knew which brands of cat food were the most popular.

However, I was looking for a companion for our daughter, not a zoology lesson.

I had been told that Baby was one year old and, although he had all of his shots, we would have to have him neutered.

A short time after Baby had become acclimated to our house, we entertained six house guests from Michigan, all cat lovers.

Baby, who had spent all of his life indoors, loved the attention he received from the houseful of company. After a few days, it appeared that he perhaps loved it too much.

He developed a strong shoe fetish and it quickly developed to the point where he became unreasonably possessive of every shoe in the house. He also began making romantic overtures to one of the guest's feet.

Our guests confirmed what we were beginning to suspect: it was time to take the worry out of being close for one particular cat.

An appointment was made with a local veterinary clinic, and, as Baby's rendezvous with destiny drew nearer, all of the humans wrestled with the moral dilemmas involved.

Someone suggested that on his last night as a male, he should be allowed to run outside. Quite interestingly, the suggestion was made by a male.

After much debate, it was decided that, in this cat's case, it would be better to lose than ever to have loved at all.

One guest told the group about a cartoon, which depicted a dog leaning out a car window, telling another dog, "Guess what, Biff? I'm being taken to the vet clinic and I'm going to be tutored!"

On Friday, Baby was taken to the clinic for his tutoring. After the cat had been given a general anesthetic, the veterinarian made two startling discoveries. Baby was four or five, not one, and he had already had the necessary alterations.

It was a day of revelation for all of us. The lovable cat has since re-established its domain over our household. We have adjusted to the fact that it will most likely continue to have a fondness for shoes and bare feet for the rest of its life.

As I mentioned before, I don't know much about male cats, but I'm learning.

We've come a long way, Baby.

The Top Secret Roller Coaster

It sounds like another Trivial Pursuit question.

How many Kuwaiti roller coasters were dismantled and moved to Baghdad by Iraqians after the August, 1990 invasion?

The answer: one.

It's true, according to the Harper's Index, published by Harper's Magazine.

Like millions of other Americans, I was glued to the television set during Operation Desert Storm. While "scuds", "sorties" and "patriot anti-missile missiles" became part of our everyday vocabulary, not once did we hear any news commentaries about missing roller coasters.

I can't recall hearing CNN's Peter Arnett describe miles of roller coaster tracks being driven on a large flatbed trailer past his hotel.

"This is Peter Arnett in Baghdad. Words can't describe the brilliant colors of the roller coaster cars being transported just outside my window. The vibrant blues, yellows and reds are absolutely spectacular in the hot noonday sun. This is the most thrilling moment of my well-publicized career."

Instead, we heard about baby formula factories and tracking missiles and we watched press briefings with weak plots. Obviously, the same people who decided to take my favorite TV programs, "Mr. Ed" and "My Mother the Car", off the air, decided not to cover the roller coaster heist. It wouldn't make sense to give the viewing public what it wanted to see.

Come to think of it, I can't remember seeing one tilt-a-whirl or ferris wheel in a John Wayne war movie. Not once did a leading man growl, "Okay, men, let's take that merry-go-round!" Instead, they opted for hills or beaches.

The roller coaster incident had to be more than a coincidence. Wars have been started over much less. Imagine the uproar in this country if Disney World or Disneyland were to disappear.

While the world's greatest minds pondered whether the war was fought because of threatened democracy or the acquisition of a major oil field, roller coasters were the last things on their minds.

Could it be that we went through all of that trouble over some metal tracks and some deep-seated desire to improve an amusement park in Baghdad? It's possible.

While people in other countries may live in constant fear of having their theme parks invaded and reduced to vacant fields, I sleep soundly at night. It makes me proud to be an American.

Females: The Deadlier of the Species

A Senate panel recently considered whether or not military women should be sent into combat.

During the hearings, retired Gen. Robert H. Barrow, a former Marine Corps commandant, observed that women can't kill in combat situations.

"It's uncivilized and women can't do it," he testified. "Women give life, sustain life, nurture life, they can't take it. If you want to make a combat unit ineffective, assign women to it."

I beg to differ. Given the right situation, any civilized woman has the capacity to be reduced to a homicidal maniac.

I know because I'm a woman and I've been there. Quite amazingly, each murderous thought had something to do with giving, sustaining or nurturing life.

During the final stage of labor, just seconds before a baby is born, ask any woman how she feels about men, particularly her husband. If she says something flowery about him, she is either lying or she has been so heavily sedated that she is unaccountable for her words or deeds.

That's why, for many years, women's arms were strapped to the delivery tables during the process of giving birth. People weren't afraid the patient would fall off the table, but rather, the straps were there for the husband's protection.

Any woman who has given birth can relate to the female crayfish, who bites off the male's head immediately after mating with him.

My primary way of nurturing and sustaining children is by buying groceries for them.

When I'm standing in a checkout line with a loaded grocery cart, and a woman in front of me decides that she has to run back and retrieve a dozen more items from the shelves, my mind is not filled with pure thoughts. While she dashes from one aisle to another, and I'm left with a gallon of melting ice cream in my cart and a checker with an apologetic look on her face, it's easy to understand how wars begin.

Whether it's a parent-teacher conference gone sour, a child left sitting on the bench for an entire sports season or some other unpleasant situation, a mother will go to any lengths to defend her children. It's part of our genetic makeup.

If women can return triumphant from an all-day, half-price sale at a shopping mall, there's no reason to doubt how they would do in military combat, crawling under barbed wire and dodging land mines.

Given the opportunity to save 50 percent, women have been known to leap over clothes racks in single bounds and to struggle to the finish over a single item of clothing. In fact, military combat might be easier. Wars have rules.

Perhaps the retired general has spent too much time in the trenches, and not enough time with good books. I would suggest that he read Rudyard Kipling, who once wrote, "The female of the species is more deadly than the male."

Dessert Life Hardships

The newspaper article left me with mixed feelings.

Published in a weekly newspaper somewhere in Iowa, the article described the return of a soldier from Operation Desert Storm. However, one sentence in particular piqued my interest.

It read, "Because (the soldier's name)'s unit was trained for woodland environment, they had to prepare for dessert life."

On one hand, I now know what it means when people say, "An army travels on its stomach." Given the opportunity to defend democracy and hot fudge sundaes, I would have gladly worn those busy, little camouflage prints.

Ever since my birth, I have been prepared for combat in a dessert life. To paraphrase an old advertising slogan, "I would gladly walk a mile for a caramel."

I have been known to fight to the finish over a last sliver of German chocolate cake or the last crumbs of a pie. Most of my brothers and sisters grew up with fork tine imprints on the backs of their hands.

Because of their early training in vanilla warfare, they will still ask everyone, including strangers in the street, if they would like dessert before taking any for themselves.

The article also brought bittersweet memories of my days as a newspaper editor. Almost a decade ago, I grew weary of teaching and inhaling endless quantities of chalk dust. I sought a more exciting career. When the local newspaper advertised an opening for an editor, I jumped at the opportunity.

Because I had just turned 40, I figured that I might as well start at the top. After all, I had all the necessary credentials - I loved writing and I had read most of the Superman comic books. Rather than settling for the role of Lois Lane, I would be Perry White.

After a short time, it became obvious that I would never win the Pulitzer Prize for journalism. It's difficult to make a national impact with recounts of county commissioner meetings, descriptions of weddings and obituaries.

However, on one occasion, I did mention that a woman had preceded in her husband in death. When she flew into the office, waving the newspaper clipping above her head, I quickly discerned the difference between fact and fiction.

Perhaps my most humbling experience of all was when the newspaper set out to publish a series of recipes using beef. One recipe described how to make beef sausage, and it should have read, "Wrap in plastic and refrigerate." In one of those irretrievable moments in journalism, a "c" was substituted for the "w" in "wrap".

Every copy of the newspaper was sold out within hours and the local post office became a mob scene as customers sent copies of the beef sausage recipe to friends and relatives from one coast to another.

In light of the recipe, my creative accounts of new tax levies and zoning regulations paled by comparison.

In one way, I had finally made a national impact. In another, I missed the sweet scent of chalk dust.

The Other Side of World Records

I like to read about people setting world records. Learning about a town that has baked the world's largest pizza or a man who has a ball of twine the size of the moon helps keep everything else in perspective.

Although none of the records broken in our home will be found in the Guiness Book of World Records, they are still noteworthy.

Because showers are taken on a non-stop basis in our house, I have seen the same bath towel washed, dried, folded and thrown back down the clothes chute five times in one day.

I've combined ground beef and cream of mushroom soup in 8,143 different recipes and they have all tasted the same.

I've gained and lost at least two tons during the past 30 years.

However, when it comes to setting new records, I must bow to the 61-year-old woman in Chile who is expecting her 65th child.

If Leontina Espinoza finds the strength and time to produce five more children, she will top the last birthathon, which was established in 1782 by a Russian woman. Apparently that woman was so busy raising 69 children that she never learned to say "nyet".

An AP release about the Chilean mother-of-all-mothers noted that the woman and her husband live in a shack 90 miles south of Santiago.

Their living conditions are understandable. The Chilean couple would truly be setting an amazing world record if they had 65 children and were still solvent.

When our first daughter was born, statistics indicated that it would cost $100,000 to raise her through four years of higher education. We had no way of knowing that four years of higher education meant fourth grade.

Picking out names for 65 children would seem like an insurmountable task. Handing out numbers would make much more sense.

"Of course we love you, 38."

"Forty-one, how many times have we told you to pick up your dirty clothes?"

It's mind-boggling to imagine how many diapers the woman has washed and how many places she has to set at the table. Receiving 65 cards on Mother's Day would seem like meager compensation for all of the work involved.

I wonder if Leontina has second thoughts about having such a large family. If her intent was to see her name in print, it might have been much easier to collect a ball of twine.

Blest be the Girdle that Binds

You can place the blame on Madonna. She was one of the first to wear unmentionables in public.

Blame also belongs to the fashion industry, which has always placed glitz ahead of comfort. As evidence of this truth, I would remind you of the pointed-toe heels of the 1950s, which allowed room for only one toe in the front of the shoe.

That small error in judgement created an entire generation of women with overlapping toes and permanent limps.

Blame anyone you want, but girdles are making a comeback after a 30-year absence. For three decades women have been told by the fashion industry that it's all right to let it all hang out. We are now being told to pull it all back in.

A spokesman for the garment industry noted that the girdle will be given more appealing names: hip slips, body shapers and body slimmers.

Call them what they might, it's not unlike referring to a guillotine as a neck enhancer or a body shortener.

If the comeback of the girdle becomes a reality, we are taking several steps backwards in our quest for a kinder, gentler nation. Instead of a thousand points of light, every woman who succumbs to the girdle fad will know a thousand points of pain.

We will finally understand the expression, "lean and mean."

An article in the *Des Moines Register* noted, "Even those with sleek, fashion-hugging bodies are gravitating towards girdles, as evidenced by teens in the size three to five range who are desperately seeking slim hips."

That's astounding. I didn't know size threes had hips. If you doubt this, check out your daughter's or granddaughter's Barbie doll. Her legs extend straight up to her shoulder blades.

Before a woman rushes off to purchase one of the new garments, she should know a few things about them.

Girdles defy gravity and compress bodies to the point where the navel rubs against the spine. Resembling a tourniquet, a girdle displaces fat, skin and vital organs to spaces above and below the garment.

In addition to posing some discomfort for the girdle wearer, this relocation naturally causes some concern for surgeons, who are unaccustomed to removing an appendix from a kneecap.

It's safe to say that women won't take the new fad sitting down. They won't be able to walk, bend over or sit down - but they will look svelte, even if they have to be propped up against walls and furniture when they're tired of standing.

The girdle comeback is a bad idea. It would be much better for a woman to wear three or four sets of shoulder pads. If she looks like the Incredible Hulk from the waist up, no one will notice her hips.

Fish Leather

Leather made from fish skin is in. Can anti-scale people be far behind?

As you read this, workers in Atlanta are handpicking scales from the skins of Alaskan salmon, Nile perch, grouper and carp. After the scales have been removed and the natural fish oils have been replaced with unscented oils, the end product is a pliable, soft and patterned leather.

Costing $16 a square foot, the leather is used for small items like belts, purses and wallets. One designer has created a swimsuit from it and a furniture maker has covered one of its chairs with the leather.

We can only wonder if a swimsuit made of fish leather would improve one's swimming abilities.

I would presume that the latter product is an arm chair and not a rocker. No one would want to risk tipping the scales.

Now that most exotic animal leathers are taboo in our society, it was only natural that fish would be considered next.

The idea of wearing fish leather does have one redemptive aspect. Someone has finally found a practical use for carp.

Once someone handed me a chunk of smoked carp and dared me to eat it. I was naturally suspicious. I'm always suspicious when I'm told that what I'm about to eat tastes like something else.

"Take a bite of this turtle meat - it tastes just like chicken."

"If you fry this venison with 10 pounds of sliced onions and add a can of mushroom soup, it will taste just like beef."

You get the picture. Rather than imagine that the alligator, rattlesnake or frog meat is chicken, I would rather have the real thing. Like many other people, I can't do two things - chew and imagine - at the same time.

On a taste scale, the carp ranked right up there with corrugated cardboard and rice cakes.

Once they have been transformed into purses and shoes, carp might finally get the approval they have been rightfully denied for so long.

If this fish leather craze catches on, I do worry about the future of leisure-time fishing. While fur trappers and furriers have been receiving all sorts of negative attention recently from the anti-fur people, what's going to keep the same thing from happening to Saturday fishermen?

Once the public is exposed to anti-scale posters showing faces of carp, with their large, unblinking eyes, will the scales (pun intended) be turned?

Will buckets of red paint be dumped on unsuspecting bullhead and carp fishermen as they watch their bobbers from roadside bridges? Let's face it. When it comes to public criticism, pan fishermen have until now remained relatively unscathed.

If worst comes to worst, and an anti-scale movement is formed, we may be reduced to a diet of turtles and rattlesnakes. I hear they taste like chicken.

Grocery Shopping

A recent survey in Progressive Grocer magazine revealed the top five priorities of grocery shoppers. Pleasant checkout clerks came fourth on the list, following cleanliness, clearly labeled prices and good produce.

My responses would have differed considerably. If I dash off to the store for a can of mushroom soup for a casserole that's supposed to be on the dinner table in half an hour, I really don't care if the can is covered with cobwebs or a year's worth of dust.

Let's face it -shopping for groceries is an eat-or-die, necessary evil, not an aesthetic experience. All I really need is a few kind words at the checkout line and fast service. If even condemned killers can be offered these two courtesies at their executions, why shouldn't they be available to innocent grocery shoppers?

When I'm in a hurry, it's often my misfortune to be standing behind a long line of customers who consider grocery shopping to be a social experience. As the ice cream melts and the potatoes begin to sprout in my cart, they use valuable time, sorting through massive files of cents-off coupons, debating whether to get the sugar bowl or the set of stainless steel cookware with their punch cards, or scratching off the numbers on their instant lottery tickets.

For these reasons, I would suggest that grocery stores implement social lanes. They would also be ideal for customers who wish to talk about the weather or to compare rainfall measurements for the last two decades.

A few of the expressions often used by checker should also be reconsidered.

"Did you find everything?" This question is an invitation to certain death. There is little possibility that I would stand in line with a loaded cart, in front of a large, tattooed man, who is carrying a case of beer, and ask for the locations of sugar and baking soda. Does the checker seriously expect us to abandon our carts at the head of a line filled with screaming children and homicidal shoppers while we run back and pick up additional items?

There's no court in the land that would convict the people left standing in line. I suspect that checkers ask the question because, like everyone else, they need a little drama in their lives.

"Do you have coupons?" Of course, working women in particular have nothing better to do with their time than browse through magazines in search of 10 cents-off coupons. In my schedule, clipping coupons ranks right up there with removing unsightly wax buildup and cleaning behind the refrigerator.

"Can you carry these, ma'am?" This question is especially disconcerting when the only item in the sack is a bag of marshmallows. Admittedly, buying groceries can be an exhausting experience, but do we look that weak to the checkers?

"Have a nice day!" After carrying a foot-long grocery list through countless aisles and accumulating a bill similar to the national debt by the time they reach the checkout counter, shoppers have good reasons to feel plundered and pillaged.

Forget the nice day. A simple "I'm sorry" would seem much more appropriate.

Putting the Bite on Dieters

It's not easy living in a state with 10,000 taxes.

This year, Minnesota legislators are preparing to tax smokers, drinkers, boaters, readers and users of cellular telephones. All of these proposals are referred to as "yuppie taxes."

However, the State Senate almost went one step too far recently when a provision was made to tax weight loss services. Evidently the suggestion tilted the scales and died on the Senate floor.

It was a clear-cut case of biting the hand that feeds. This wasn't what we had in mind when we told our legislators to go after the fat in state government.

Unlike cigarettes, where Minnesotans can drive into another state and buy their smokes for less money, I can't imagine driving 100 miles into another state just to be weighed and be told that you still have to lose another 40 pounds. A person can only take so much abuse.

Before the idea of a weight loss tax comes up again, it would only make sense to have an environmental impact study made. If Minnesotans would bulk at the new weight loss tax, they might also affect the destiny of the world.

If this seems preposterous, consider the following scenario.

Given the choice of paying the tax or not paying the tax, most people, myself included, would go off their diets completely. As a direct result, countless additional tons of junk food would be shipped into the state on a weekly basis.

The weight of the junk food, combined with the additional weight on each man, woman and child, would make Minnesota one of the heaviest areas of the world.

We should be reminded at this point that a piece of sour cream chocolate cake weighs considerably more than a leaf of lettuce or a cube of tofu.

Instead of being known as the state of 10,000 lakes, we would be recognized as the state with the 10,000-pounds-a-week weight gain.

Given the disproportionate weight in one geographical area, it might be possible for the world to be thrown off its delicate axis. Losing its usual momentum, the planet could go spiralling off into space to who knows where.

Our unexpected relocation in the galaxy would make the greenhouse effect seem like a relatively minor problem, to say nothing of unsightly dishwasher spots and bad breath.

The provision was a bad idea. By imposing a weight loss tax, the legislators would be conveying the message, "Let them eat cake." And we would.

Curb Service Psychologists

A Manhattan psychotherapist now offers curb service to her clients.

Rather than having her clients drive across town to sort out their problems, she picks them up in her mobile office - a 35-foot white limousine, complete with a sun roof, bar, stereo and television.

Including a cruise around town, 55 minutes of therapy can cost $130, plus another $60 for the limousine rental. The most amazing fact is that she already has 30 mobile patients. The newspaper article describing the new service explained that the patients are short on time, but long on cash and troubles.

I can only imagine what effect the service would have on my hometown - population 4,800.

If the psychotherapist's limousine was to make a housecall in this town, one of several assumptions would be made:

1. Someone was having car trouble on the nearby interstate. It's safe to say that, except for car troubles, people only turn off at our town's exit if they have a special purpose in mind. Whether that purpose is to sell a load of cattle, to buy groceries or to visit a relative, they drive directly from one spot to another. There aren't too many stretch limousines casually cruising up and down our streets.

2. A white stretch limousine might suggest to some people that someone in town was trying to outdo everyone else with a fancier-than-usual funeral. When it comes to a town this size, that kind of uppityness isn't taken lightly.

3. Other people might presume that some Hollywood actor or rock star was returning to his or her roots. While some folks might try to figure out

whether their second-cousin's daughter might have become Madonna, others would be debating whether a street should be renamed in his or her honor or if it would be more appropriate to present the visiting celebrity with an oversized key to the city. In less time than you can say the words, "Add one can of cream of celery soup," at least three potluck dinners would be scheduled to celebrate the occasion. After all, if Donna Reed came back to her small Iowa hometown, why shouldn't our town be next?

4. A more terrifying assumption would be that the car belongs to some drug baron or a member of organized crime. Our town may not be large, but we do watch prime-time television.

5. If news about the Manhattan psychotherapist were to become public knowledge, it would be assumed that someone was having incredibly big problems. In the big city, the limousine guarantees patients a certain degree of anonymity. There are no awkward stares in waiting rooms and the limousine swims unobtrusively in a sea of other big cars.

Even if it weren't public knowledge, people would sense something was amiss. If a long limousine pulled up in a driveway and any one of us was seen for the next hour, riding aimlessly up and down the city streets, people would shake their heads in disbelief.

"So it's come to this", they would say. It's a nice blanket statement that covers every unusual situation.

Being unusual isn't taken lightly, either.

Fainting Goats

More over, potbelly pigs, and make way for fainting goats.

Now that having a domesticated pig in the house has run full circle, there's literally a new kid on the block. According to an article in the *Wall Street Journal*, fainting goats have a genetic trait that causes them to stiffen up and fall when frightened.

I once had a great-aunt who used to do the same thing.

The goats have become so popular that there's an International Fainting Goat Association. They even have a newsletter, "Fall in Love with Fainters."

Having a fainting goat might have its advantages over having a potbelly pig. I know I wouldn't be able to eat bacon or enjoy Easter hams with a porcine pet underfoot. It would somehow smack of cannibalism.

Although the comic premise that goats will eat anything, including tin cans, remains doubtful, having a pet goat would certainly solve many of our recycling problems.

We would be able to impress people by telling them about our children's nanny. Goats also have two other advantages over usual housepets, such as dogs, cats and parakeets: they can be milked and they could keep a family well-supplied with sweaters.

A fainting goat could also supply social excuses when we normally find it hard to say, "No, thank you."

Imagine if you will, the following phone conversations: "You are saying that you need four pies, six hot dishes and four dozen cookies for the bazaar tomorrow? That would be no...Wait a minute! My goat just fainted. Could I call you back?"

"I would really like to come into work today, but, you see, my goat just fainted."

A fainting goat, which can't be a pretty picture, would be the perfect excuse for leaving committee meetings running longer than three hours, or not showing up for root canal work at the dentist's office.

With any amount of luck, my pet goat would be terrified of noises produced by vacuum cleaners and washing machines and the bothersome, screeching sounds when windows are washed. If it would mean having a faint-free goat, I would gladly give up doing those tasks.

Finally, we would be able to utter the age-old expression, "You know, you get my goat!", and really mean it.

Roll out the Pork Barrel

Some people have all the fun.

While the rest of us were wrestling with our income tax forms and debating whether a box of raisin bran cereal was worth $4 at the grocery store, some folks in Washington were engaged in one of their favorite leisure time activities: pork barreling.

An article in *Time* magazine unearthed several pet porcine projects, totalling over $314 million, which slipped into various appropriations bills while we were sleeping.

More money than most of us can imagine will be spent for building a new government building in the Solomon Islands, $5 million; creating a garden in Miami, $1.36 million; renovating a catfish farm in Arkansas, $2.7 million; and a study to determine why people don't ride bicycles to work, $1 million.

I'd like to play that game.

Given $314 million, I would gladly sponsor the following bills:

Cost: $100 million. The federal government could furnish all of the return postage for our tax forms on April 15. Being asked to supply the postage stamps after we have already spent countless manhours sharpening pencils, looking for lost receipts and trying to decipher endless pages of directions, is the final insult. As William Shakespeare once noted, "This is the most unkindest cut of all."

Cost: $2 million. A study could be made to explain why eating one pound of chocolates can result in a 20-pound weight gain.

Cost: $1.6 million. A study would be conducted to

determine why it always rains after we wash our cars and why the phone inevitably rings while we're taking showers.

Cost: $3 million. An unauthorized biography could be written about Kitty Kelley.

Cost: $5 million. A comprehensive study would determine if there is any truth to the expression, "It gets better after 40".

Cost: $10 million. A plan could be implemented whereby any person would be immediately imprisoned for saying, "Have a nice day" and not meaning it.

Cost: $1 million. A study would be made to explain why Congressman Martin Sabo, Minnesota, who sponsored the aforementioned bicycle study, still drives a car to work.

The list could go on and on. Give it a try. After all, it's only other people's money.

It's a Good Wind that Brings Good News

There's one thing to be said about spring house cleaning. It's great for people who have nothing better to do with their time.

Instead of washing down walls, chasing dust balls and cleaning closets, my version of spring cleaning consists mostly of making a list of things to be done.

Once the list is written, it's placed in a conspicuous spot on the kitchen counter for all to see. Over the years my lists have impressed a legion of babysitters, milkmen and drop-in visitors.

With a bold-face heading, THINGS TO DO, the list usually includes: clear path through living room, sort out baby clothes (a sentimental favorite since our baby is now 19), and bulldoze the basement. If nothing else, my list is creative.

For all I know, St. Bernard of Clairvaux was thinking of my lists when he noted that the road to a certain warm place is paved with good intentions. In the confusion, he might well have been one of our drop-in guests.

Because of a stroke of good fortune last week, I won't have to worry about writing a fictional list this year. As strong winds blew in from the south one day, a made-to-order list was literally deposited at my doorstep. It seemed like a miracle, not unlike manna dropped from heaven.

Neatly written on lined, lavender paper, the list includes an exhausting litany of household chores. There must be at least 30 items on the list.

One which particularly struck my fancy was "paint the bathtub." Never in my wildest dreams have I thought of doing that. It would be much easier to close the shower curtains and block out the tub than to paint it.

At least 20 items on the list include painting, stripping and refinishing rooms or pieces of furniture, enough to keep the list writer busy until at least the end of this century.

We're not talking routine spring cleaning here. We're talking about a person who should perhaps cut back on her caffeine intake.

What bothers me most of all is the thought that some woman in this town has just received a semiload of paint, varnish and floor tiles and, without her list, has no idea what to do with them or where to start.

If the list writer should read this, she should know that the list is safe on my kithcen counter and she may have it back. Enough people have already been impressed.

It might also do her some good to visit our house and see how the rest of us live.

The Ultimate Vacation

According to Saddam Hussein, we have seen the "mother of all wars". Now be prepared for the "mother of all vacations".

An island paradise, Necker Island in the British Bahamas, could be rented to you and up to 19 guests. The vacation package includes meals, drinks, accomodations and various activities, including the use of a snooker table from England.

With a price tag of $9,000 a day, one can only presume that you wouldn't be served frozen microwave dinners.

It sounds like a little too much for our checkbook. Besides, I wouldn't know what to do with a snooker table if I saw one. I'm not even sure whether a person should snooker in mixed company.

The island getaway would cost $375 an hour or $6.25 a minute. In the time it would take to brush your teeth, you would have spent $31. It would be impossible to sleep, knowing that eight hours in bed would carry a $3,000 price tag.

While our daughters were still young and impressionable, we would take them on family vacations and stay in what we considered to be luxury motels. Any place that offered complimentary soap and paper strips across the toilet seat seemed really special at the time. If the motels offered in-room movies, we would pinch ourselves to make sure we weren't dreaming.

The motels usually had the words "budget" or "economy" in their names and they allowed children to stay free in the same room with their parents, allowing for maximum togetherness. In most cases, they were conveniently located near a cluster of gas stations off an interstate.

If the motel had an indoor pool, we thought we were living a life of luxury. For extra excitement, our daughters were content to ride for hours on the motel elevators. Their other diversions included running the ice machine and checking pay telephones for forgotten quarters.

We would make side trips to superlative attractions: the world's largest pile of used car tires, the world's largest plaster dinosaur. We would only eat at restaurants with golden arches.

As we drove from one motel stop to another, we would sing songs and play billboard games for hours. We would keep a detailed account of out-of-state license plates as if the future of the world depended upon it.

If our repertoire of 3,000 childhood songs became exhausted, our daughters would signal from the car's back window and semi-truck drivers would sound their air horns.

In retrospect, they were wonderful vacations. As our car became filled with fast-food wrappers, souvenirs made in Taiwan and heated arguments about who would sit next to the window, we didn't know about islands in the British Bahamas.

We felt rich, anyway.

Recycling Sounds Like Exercise

Recycling sounded like a bad idea at first. Because it's such an active verb, I thought it had something to do with exercise.

Now that recycling has become a household word, I'm a believer. Let's face it...anything that has to do with food containers can't be all bad.

This year, all residents of our town were given containers in which to store plastics, glass containers, metals, newsprint and corrugated cardboard. We were also given sheets of instructions, roughly the length of a short novel, to study carefully. I only hope there isn't a test.

Ostensibly, every resident who has read the directions knows everything there is to know about recycling. We should understand the chemical composition of various plastics and glass products. No questions should be left unanswered.

Wrong. Some aspects of recycling still bother me.

For example, we have been told to rinse out all metal cans and plastic containers.

Last week I tried rinsing out a plastic liquid laundry detergent bottle until it was free of all residue. During the seemingly endless project, I must have used up 500 gallons of running water. As soap bubbles kept appearing for the longest time, I wondered: Are the water conservationists aware of what the recyclists are doing?

In order to prepare the plastic bottle for recycling, I used enough water to save at least three fruit orchards in California or to provide enough bath water for a medium sized city.

It would be much less wasteful if we would take those cans and bottles, which need to be rinsed, into the showers with us. Not only would this idea save large quantities of water, but it would also give us something to do between our shampoos and cream rinses.

Something else troubles me about recycling: what do we do with the grease leftover from frying bacon and hamburgers? For all of my adult life, I have poured the hot grease into a sealed coffee can, which is stored under the kitchen sink. By doing so, the drains wouldn't be clogged. It was a family tradition followed by my mother and her mother before her.

Now that coffee cans have been determined to be recyclable, I have no place to go with the grease. Last week, I tried pouring the hot grease into other containers: a styrofoam cup which had once held coleslaw and a paper milk carton.

After pouring the grease into the cup, I was left with the mother of all messes on the countertop. While the grease escaped in all directions, the cup resembled a glob of melted marshmallow. A roll of paper toweling saved the day.

The paper milk container was also an exercise in futility. As grease spurted through the seams and tiny holes invisible to the naked eye, I cleaned the mess up with another roll of paper toweling.

Do the save-the-trees people know what the recyclists are doing?

One thing's for certain. When it comes to recycling, I still have much to learn.

Runners aren't Sociable

There's good news for those rare individuals who wear sweatbands and could care less whether they ever see another piece of chocolate.

It turns out that if you run about a mile and a half every day, you get fewer head colds.

As far as many of us are concerned, we might as well be told to stand on our heads or do back flips. We aren't designed for rapid movement.

It's not that I don't run. I dash off to the grocery store. I run to the post office. I run to the bank. The only difference between my running and the running done by a marathon participant is that I use a car.

I tried running one day in 1972, while on a health kick that mercifully was short-lived. During the 1½-mile course, which aged me by five years and lasted most of a morning, I discovered more than I wanted to know about my body's main muscle groups and the principles of hyperventilation.

By the time I had dragged myself halfway home, I experienced a startling revelation: People are divided into two distinct groups - runners and non-runners.

The reason why runners have fewer head colds is easy to explain. We catch colds from contact with other people. While a runner is kicking up dust on lonely country roads or doing laps on a deserted track, there's little opportunity for socialization. Runners simply have less exposure to other people.

When you're running alone with the wind, it's not very likely that people will cough or sneeze in your face. It's the isolation, not the exercise, that keeps runners from having head colds.

Think about it. Have you ever seen a runner stop suddenly and pass the time of day with another person? When was the last time a runner stopped at the local bakery to have a few doughnuts and some good conversation and share a few sneezes?

If runners should say that it feels good to have their lungs bursting through their rib cages and to have their calves feel like knotted ropes, they would probably lie about other things. Physical pain can't be that enjoyable.

I, for one, would rather be a sociable non-runner than a non-sociable runner.

I would also miss the doughnuts.

Colorado: The Good Food State

Colorado must be a nice place to live - especially if you're leafy, green or yellow.

While its sister states wrestle with issues like human rights and deficit budgets, Colorado has gone where no state has gone before. A bill passed by its legislature on February 4, 1991, prohibits anyone from making disparaging remarks about perishable fruit, vegetable and dairy products. The bill awaits final approval by the state senate.

State Representative Steve Acquafresca, who also moonlights as a consultant to fruit growers, drafted the bill on the heels of the 1989 controversy over Alar-sprayed apples. The situation no doubt worsened when President Bush publicly made defamatory comments about broccoli.

The *Time* article about the bill didn't mention any penalties connected to bad-mouthing agricultural products, but I can't imagine anyone doing hard labor for making insidious remarks about lima beans. It's unclear whether the bill pertains to public figures, the media or private individuals.

One can only assume that people in Colorado will no longer be referred to as "couch potatoes" or "bad apples". Red-haired people will no longer be "carrot heads" and embarrassed people will not be "red as a beet''. You would certainly think twice before calling someone a "milquetoast''.

Carried to an extreme, the bill could certainly eliminate the problem of crowded classrooms. I doubt whether there is anyone under the age of 12 who hasn't said something negative about food, whether it be brussel sprouts or school cafeteria food in general.

Imagine, if you will, this scenario:

Johnny Smith, age 10, has been dawdling at the dinner table. While everyone else at the table has been eating, he has been playing with the food on his plate, creating a volcano out of the pile of cottage cheese and standing the broccoli spears on end so they look like a forest of small trees.

"Johnny, eat your food,'' admonishes his mother.

"But, Mom, I ha..''

Don't say it!'' screams his father, waving his fork for added emphasis.

"But I hate...''

"Don't say it!'' shouts his family in unison. Over the years, they have all grown rather fond of Johnny.

"I hate this food,'' Johnny mutters.

Johnny's father, looking downcast, walks to the phone and dials the hotline number, 555-FOOD. He is put on hold as his call is processed. Because it's dinnertime, the phone lines are jammed as civic-minded citizens call the hotline about refusals to eat chopped liver, cooked cabbage and lima beans.

"I hate to do this to you, son,'' Johnny's father tells him, "but it's the law.''

I'm happy there were no such laws when I was growing up. Because of my lifelong aversion to asparagus, I would still be making license plates.

Wish You were Hair

When people return from vacations, they often have a certain glow.

Whether it comes from hours spent in the sun in Texas or Florida, or it's merely their blood pressure short-circuiting after too many stops at fast food restaurants, the glow is there.

If current plans being made by Russia's Kiev-turist are realized, there might be another reason. The Ukrainian tour operator is organizing excursions to the radioactive ruins of Chernobyl, the site of the world's worst nuclear accident.

It's one more example of how truth can be stranger than fiction.

Although Soviet scientists are still conducting tests to make sure tourists will not suffer incidental side effects, like shortened lifespans or falling hair, tours are set to begin in about a month.

It may soon be possible for vacationers to return home, loaded down with not only postcards and snapshots, but also with new hairdos and built-in lighting systems for their homes because of their ability to glow in the dark.

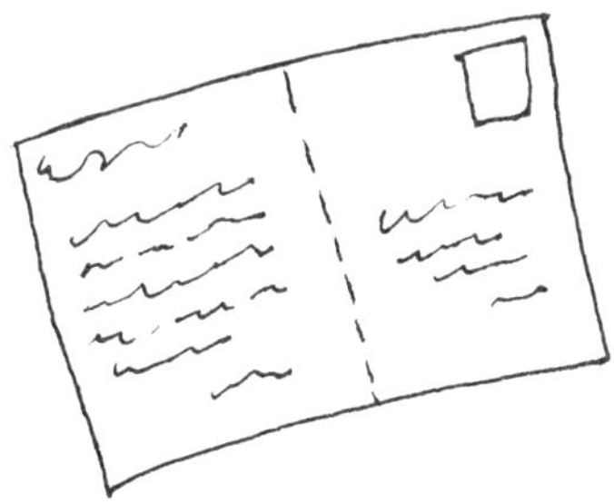

Perhaps the tourism folks in my county could follow the creative example set by the Soviets. Although we don't have a disaster site to lure tourists off the interstate, we do have one proud claim to fame: we're apparently the only county in Minnesota without a lake.

If tourists are willing to pay $4 a day to view the buried wreckage of a nuclear reactor, we also might have some possibilities. Perhaps we should take a second look at our state-of-the-art sewage treatment facilities or the settling ponds next to the meat processing plant. For the feint-hearted, there's also our local buffalo herd at the state park.

At least people's vacation photos would turn out after visiting our county, which is more than can be said for Chernobyl.

If you have ever traveled to a foreign country, perhaps you've had film overexposed in one of those airport x-ray scanners. If it's true that thousands of residents are still being moved out of Chernobyl's contaminated zones, it's also possible that your film could be exposed before you even have a chance to remove your camera's lens cap.

One of the highlights of the Chernobyl tour will be a visit to a nuclear-waste dump.

On the other hand, if you would prefer to avoid needless airfare costs to Russia, I'll be glad to show you our county's landfill for $4.

Clean Underwear: Don't Leave Home Without It

Since her marriage to Prince Charles a few years ago, Princess Diana has spent an estimated $26,460 on underwear.

This little known fact was reported by *Harper's Weekly* and it can only lead to one of two conclusions about life in the throne lane. Either Princess Diana has a wonderful credit rating or she had a mother like mine while she was growing up.

My mother's most often repeated words of advice dealt with underwear. As a direct result of that advice I was given a somewhat distorted impression of the nursing profession.

"Always wear nice, clean underwear," she would admonish, shaking her finger at my nose. "If you don't, and you're in an accident and taken to the hospital, you will be terribly embarrassed, young lady." She would shake her finger again, a trick of the trade she learned in Motherhood 101.

The implication was that nurses, like *Harper's Weekly*, have little to do with their time other than talk about other people's underwear. Evidently, whether or not a person is wearing torn underwear or an inferior brand could determine his or her medical care while in the hospital.

Tattered underwear could be a matter of life or death.

"Paging Dr. Jones...paging Dr. Jones. Please report to the lovely Fruit of the Looms in room 224."

"Honestly, Madge, did you see the underwear that just came through the emergency room?"

"We would really like to give you a transfusion, Sir, but the stretched-out waistband on your boxer shorts is a real turn-off for all of us on the staff."

Over the years, I've met quite a few nurses and not once have our conversations turned to underwear. On the job, they usually talk about vital signs and diets and they use long Latin words with at least four syllables. Not once have I been led to believe that the level of medical care is determined by the status of one's underwear.

In the case of my mother, I only need to consider the source. She also told me that if I crossed my eyes they would stay that way and a sweaty sock wrapped around my neck overnight would cure a sore throat.

Actually, in spite of the fact that wrapping a sweaty sock around my throat made me smell like a locker room and curbed my social life, it did work.

In an ironic twist of fate, I became my mother. When the time came to send our daughters out into the world, I told them about crossed eyes and nice, clean underwear. Like my mother and her mother before her, I shook my finger at their noses.

I can only presume Princess Diana is doing the same with her sons.

This Restaurant has my Tongue

Montrachet, a chic restaurant in New York City, now offers lamb's tongue salad at $9 a serving.

Not to be outdone, other upscale restaurants throughout the country are selling calf-brain pancakes ("crepes de cervelle de veau"), calf glands ("grilled sweetbreads"), and cattle stomach lining stew ("tripe").

It's enough to make a person think twice before accepting a dinner invitation. It also gives new meaning to the expression, "You are what you eat."

I may be old fashioned, but I'm reluctant to eat vital organs, even if there are cloth napkins on the table. My fear of the unknown extends to foods which move on my plate. For the first six years of my life, I refused to eat jello because it shimmied and quivered. I was convinced it was alive.

My mother, recognizing that my refusal to eat jello would eventually lead to a refusal to eat unusual foods later in life, used the only child psychology available to parents in the mid-1940s.

She threatened to kill me. I was surprised when the jello didn't scream out in pain with the first bite.

Thanks to her intervention, I was willing to try raw oysters later in life.

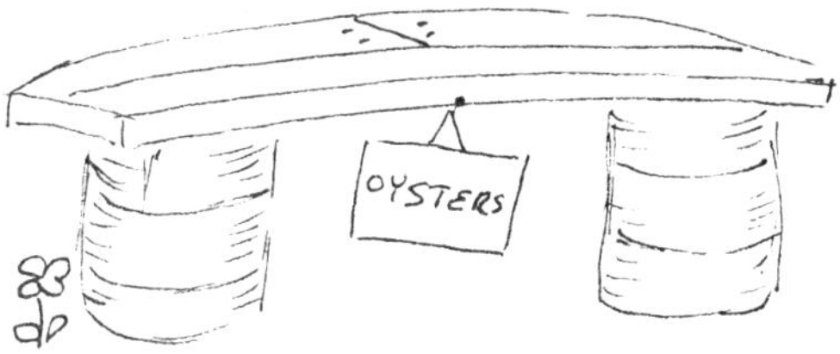

It happened several years ago while my husband and I were visiting New Orleans. We discovered an oyster bar on a street corner in the French Quarter. My husband, a more adventurous eater, decided that our lives wouldn't be complete without the dubious delicacies.

The food stall lacked ambience - it consisted of long, unfinished boards strung across two oil drums. The man in charge wore a rubber apron and he kept busy splitting open oyster shells with a knife and slipping their contents onto crackers for appreciative customers.

"Want to try some?" he asked, wiping the large knife across his apron. My husband, the risk taker, agreed to try the first one. The man with the knife said the best way to eat an oyster was on a cracker with a dash of tabasco sauce.

"Chew it two or three times and then swallow," he told my husband.

I was offered the second oyster. The shapeless blob sat on the cracker and resembled gray jello. I chewed it twice and swallowed.

I had expected the oyster to feel slimy and to taste like brackish backwater. Instead, it tasted simply watery.

"That was good," I lied to the man with the knife. "But tell me, when did that oyster actually die? When it was pulled from its shell or when it was pulled from the sea?"

The man gave me a smile and I noticed that a substantial number of his teeth were missing. He gave the knife another swipe across his apron as he spoke.

"When did it die? The first time you bit into it," he laughed.

I laughed too. It's a good idea to laugh when the oyster man, seeking approval, has a knife in his hand.

Rudy's Portrait

Let's give the guy a break.

Former Minnesota Governor Rudy Perpich would like to have a second portrait hung in the state capitol. He reasons that he's entitled to it because he served two non-consecutive terms as the state's chief executive.

Since his first portrait was hung, he has darker hair, he's lost several pounds and he wears different glasses.

Like most of us, Rudy is looking for that one perfect photo.

His request merely underlines something I've believed for years: within each of us lies the potential for one perfect marriage, one perfect diet and one perfect photo.

Fortunately, I've already had one of each.

My one ideal diet took place two years ago. After drinking huge amounts of water, actually the equivalent of Lake Superior, and consuming at least 1,000 heads of lettuce, I became a shadow of my former self.

In light of that success, I doubt whether I would ever be able to do it again.

The diet's downfall occurred when I decided that within each of us also lies the potential to eat one perfect hot fudge sundae. From that moment on, my diet became history and my search for the perfect combination of ice cream, hot fudge and chopped nuts relentlessly continues.

My perfect photo was taken in 1959, a few months

before I graduated from high school. It's the one photo with which I would like to be remembered.

I can't be sure, but I think I started aging within seconds of that sitting. The photographer, apparently taken aback at my natural beauty, nevertheless was shooting for realism. By the time the finished photos were returned to me, he had added a cowlick to my short hair and a few blemishes to my face. There were also some other imperfections not worth mentioning.

To his credit, he fell short of adding birthmarks and a scar running the full length of my face.

Although it was my best photo, I landed up looking like all of my classmates. As far as my natural beauty was concerned, only my photographer knew for sure.

While Rudy Perpich's hairdresser may be the only one who knows for sure why the former governor's hair turned darker over a period of 12 years, I think the man should be given another portrait.

This one might be perfect.

E-X-C-U-S-E Me!

This is one of the times when I'm glad I'm not a cow.

Three researchers from Washington State University will be receiving a total of $210,000 from the Federal Environmental Protection Agency to study cow burps and how the methane gases they produce contribute to the greenhouse effect. It's believed that about 15 percent of the methane released into the atmosphere comes from ruminant animals.

Hundreds of cows will be outfitted with gas monitors that measure their belches. How humiliating.

Outside of mentioning that an additional 20 percent of the methane is produced by natural wetlands, nothing was said in the article I read about the sources of the other 65 percent. The whole article made me pretty uneasy, because I can sense where this project is heading.

I've known quite a few belchers in my time, and they weren't cows. If this project goes much further, the EPA will be seeking out two-legged culprits.

Customers of restaurants serving Mexican food and other spicy foods might be subjected to belchalizer tests, not unlike the breathalizer tests already in existence.

Imagine, if you will, the following scenario:

A couple, Mary and John, have just left their favorite Mexican restaurant when they're stopped outside the door by two ominous-looking men, wearing government-issue trenchcoats and flashing shiny EPA badges.

"Just where do you think you're going?" growls one of the men, as he grabs John by the lapels of his overcoat.

"H-o-m-e," stammers John. "Our babysitter has to be home by 10 and we promised not to be late."

"This won't take long," states the second man, as he produces two face masks equipped with sensors and small guages.

"What's this all about?" asks John, his courage slowly returning. "Honestly, we didn't have anything to drink except coffee."

"Don't play coy with us," snaps the first man. "My partner and I watched you through the window. We saw you eat the frijoles refritos. We watched you dip your way through two servings of picante sauce. In only a matter of time, both of you will be endangering our planet with your belches."

John and Mary struggle as the masks are slipped over their faces.

"You really don't understand, do you?" the man continues. "If you keep eating spicy foods, our planet will gradually get warmer. When things get really bad, we'll be having winters with 70-degree temperatures!"

Hearing this, John, who has had his car jump-started already three times this winter and has had his ears frozen twice, tears off his mask, grabs his wife and heads back into the restaurant. He orders double servings of refried beans and dreams of warmer weather.

Once the researchers determine how much methane gas should be attributed to cow belches, we can only wonder what changes will be made.

Perhaps the cows will be put on a bland diet of oatmeal or they will be required to cover their mouths with their hooves when burping.

I wouldn't know. Ask the guys getting the $210,000.

Boomers Cover Up

According to sources in the clothing industry, baby boomers are once more covering up for two reasons: heating bills and embarrassment. It seems their children are now old enough to begin staring.

The *Wall Street Journal* noted, "The Woodstock generation didn't believe in wearing things to bed, and pajamas fell into disrepute."

Because I missed being a baby boomer for four years and a world war, I've always worn something to bed. My principle concern has been that the house would burn down in the middle of the night and I would be left standing in the street wearing only a smile. There I would stand, surrounded by grinning firemen and neighbors bringing over casseroles.

For 28 Christmases, I've been convinced that each year's tree would cause the big fire. Extension cords and burning candles are other sources of constant anxiety. I'm a lot of fun during the holidays.

Because of my fear of house fires, I always go to bed fully covered. I also figure that in the time that it would take me to get dressed and jump out a window, my husband could lead our children to safety and I could grab my most prized possessions: my recipe file, any chocolate chips left in the cupboard and the one dress that I've been told makes me look ten pounds slimmer.

A person has to have priorities.

I haven't always worn flannel nightgowns and pajamas. For many years I wore frilly little gowns, given to me at bridal showers by friends and aunts with a flair for the romantic. I even wore them during the winters, and though my skin was covered with goose bumps and my lips turned blue, I looked nice.

Occasionally I would throw on a flannel nightgown and my husband would ask, "Don't you feel well?" He had grown accustomed to seeing me dressed like an oversized Barbie doll.

As I got older and more practical, flannel nightwear became the rule rather than the exception. Quite coincidentally, I began wearing bifocals, flannel nightgowns and control top pantyhose at the same time.

A short time ago, I threw caution to the wind and decided to wear one of those frilly gowns from long ago. My husband looked up from his evening newspaper and asked, "Don't you feel well?"

So it's back to warm flannel on these cold winter nights. By the way, where's the greenhouse effect when we could really use it?

Bad-mouthing Chocolate

It has to be a misprint. That's the only explanation for the recent newspaper article describing the evils of chocolate.

According to a press release from the Minnesota Dietetic Association and reprinted by a statewide Minnesota newspaper, the typical 12-ounce box of assorted chocolates contains 2,000 calories, "of which 1,400 are from fa(n)t(astic ingredients that are good for you)".

Undoubtedly, we will be seeing a correction very soon.

Let's look at a typical box of assorted chocolates, and I'm sure you will agree that chocolates are essential for your health and well-being.

In every assortment you will find several clumps of coconut covered with a thin layer of chocolate. If you bite into one, you will discover that between those strands of coconut there are numerous pockets of air. In addition, coconut is a fruit. Fresh air and fruit - it's a nutritionist's dream.

There are also jelly-filled chocolates. Jelly, for the record, is nothing more than thickened fruit juice. If it weren't for coconut and jelly filled chocolates, I would have succumbed to scurvy years ago.

The cream and butter found in other chocolates keep all of us from walking hunched over like Quasimoto, the legendary bell-ringer of Notre Dame. As we're told over and over again during Dairy Month, milk products are necessary for healthy bones and teeth.

Even chocolate is vastly underrated. If you will

agree that all matter on this planet is divided into three groups, animals, plants and minerals, chocolate has to be considered a vegetable. It's like brussels sprouts and carrots, only more appetizing.

We can only be led to believe that the fault lies not with chocolate, but rather the mythical calorie system. The system was most likely the brainchild of a subversive named Cal, who wished to make all humans miserably guilt-ridden. Because of him, people erroneously believe that a 12-ounce box of chocolates can add 20 pounds to a person's total weight.

Think about it. If you eat a pound of chocolate, you should only gain a pound. Eat a pound of celery, and you should have the same results. It's only logical.

In its press release, the dietetic association suggests that a healthful way to deal with chocolate is to take it to your workplace and share it with fellow employees.

It sounds like another one of Cal's crazy ideas.

Let this be a Sign

It's not that I'm unwilling to live with new ideas.

I can accept that the earth is round and that we circle the sun, rather than the other way around. I know that any purchased chocolate should be consumed within one hour.

However, when my hometown decided to change most of its stop signs, I short circuited.

It's almost a certainty that if they wouldn't have changed the signs, I wouldn't have climbed into the wrong car at the post office this week.

Once known as the city of trees, long before anyone knew about Dutch Elm Disease, our town is rapidly becoming known as the city of 10,000 stops.

I don't know who came up with the idea. Perhaps it was the same person who reorganizes grocery store shelves and aisles or the person who determines hemlines.

Stop signs were put up and others were taken down. On the first day after the changeover, I ran through at least two stop signs, leaving pedestrians huddling in the curbs and cars slamming on their breaks.

I'm not the only person affected by the newly placed signs. Not only do we have to stop for the new signs, but we also have to stop at corners where there used to be signs. Driving has become much more exciting and maneuvering the intersections is not unlike playing Pac Man. You either think fast or disappear from the screen.

My drive to the post office, four blocks away, used to require one stop, but now it requires no less than four.

One morning this week, I drove to the post office and the stop-and-go pattern simply got to me. What should have been a routine, ho-hum drive turned into a white-knuckled adventure. Other drivers were also adjusting to the unfamiliar stop signs.

By the time I had parked my car, I was completely disoriented, unable to recall my name, my social security number or the first names of my children.

Things hadn't improved much by the time I climbed back into the car and closed the door. The red interior of the car was the same, but everything else had changed. As I reached for the key in the ignition, I noticed that the radio had been relocated and the dashboard had different knobs.

I first thought the city must have changed the cars as well as the stop signs. That thought was short-lived when I realized, in a flood of panic, that I had entered the wrong car.

Hoping to avoid an encounter with the car's owner, who should be returning to the car any minute, I scooped up my belongings from the seat and made a quick exit.

It wasn't quick enough.

I had just shut the door behind me when the car's owner, a woman I had never seen before, came out of the post office. She understandably looked confused. It's not often you find a stranger leaving your parked car.

"It's the stop signs," I murmured apologetically.

She just smiled. It was the same smile you given an elderly relative who marches to a different drummer.

Not that I march to a different drummer. It was just the stop signs.

How to Know if You're Losing It

There are two "its" associated with middle age.

One "it" occurs when you turn 40 and people waving black balloons tell you, "It gets better after 40."

The only problem is that they don't explain what "it" is.

The second "it" is found in the expressions, "I'm losing it," or "You're losing it, Mom." In this case, "it" is more clearly defined. They're talking about your mind, your ability to function normally in the day-to-day world.

Magazines often have mini-quizzes for their readers about their social life: "How to Know if You've Found the Right Mate" or "How Perfect is Your Marriage?" I've yet to see a quiz that measures how much grip we've lost on the real world.

For that reason, I propose the following quiz, "How to Know When You're Losing It." If you have experienced any of the following situations, please subtract one point from a perfect score of 10. If you lose track of your score after the first few items, welcome to the club.

You know you're losing it:

When your list of "things to do today" includes getting out of bed and brushing your teeth.

When you accidentally use room spray instead of spray deodorant and you spend the rest of the day smelling like a pine forest.

When you arrive at the grocery store and discover you've left both your shopping list and your checkbook at home.

When you say one thing, but mean another.

When you not only forget the names of your children, but you also begin referring to them as "the blonde" and "the short one."

When you walk down to the basement and then forget why you went down there.

When you dial a phone number, and while it's ringing, you can't remember why you made the call.

When you can't recall where you parked your car.

When you are introducing your very best friend to another person and you completely forget your friend's name.

When you're writing a quiz for a newspaper column and you can't recall what the tenth question was supposed to be.

I must admit that I lost "it" when my birthday cakes began resembling bonfires. It no longer pains me to admit "My mind's a blank" or "I can't remember." I've grown rather used to stopping in mid-sentence and forgetting what I was talking about. I no longer lose sleep when I forget the punch lines to jokes.

Perhaps that's what people mean when they say "It gets better after 40." Your mind goes, but you don't worry about it.

The Art of Raking Leaves

Raking leaves requires perfect timing. It's not a challenge to be taken lightly or with reckless abandon.

After years of raking leaves I thought I had come up with the perfect system.

If you panic and start raking too early in the fall, you will find yourself raking at least a dozen times. If you start too late you run the risk of having to shovel the snow in order to find the leaves.

The city's pickup schedule for leaves and lawn trimmings should also be taken into consideration. Although I didn't pay much attention to the schedule this year, I believe that this year's dates for leaf pickups were set for July 15 and August 1, long before the trees were ready to shed their leaves.

Some cities also require leaves to be placed in loose piles on the curbs, where they will most likely be carried off by the wind into another county, if not recycled onto another lawn.

Other cities prefer to have leaves picked up in plastic bags. The bags are then moved by city crews to the landfill where they remain intact for at least 100 years.

I don't know about your feelings, but whenever I drive by the landfill it's somehow reassuring to realize that under that mountain of garbage and debris lie the perfectly preserved plastic bags of leaves I raked in 1984. It gives me a comforting sense of immortality.

This fall I faced leaf raking with a certain smugness. While our neighbors raked their leaves on a daily basis, dutifully meeting the designated pickup times and sacrificing their personal lives in the process, I waited until the right moment.

They had their leaves neatly wrapped up in plastic bags and placed on the curbs at the right times - by 3 a.m. on the third Monday of the month and by midnight on the second Saturday of the month. As their hands became covered with blisters from repeated rakings, I waited until the last maple leaf had fallen.

I hadn't counted on an early snowfall. By the time the day finally arrived to rake our lawn, according to my new system, the leaves were buried under snow.

While others may call it laziness or an unwillingness to comply with the system, I prefer to call it mulching the lawn.

As long as the snow remains, our lawn looks like any other. Snow tends to be a great equalizer.

The Copyright

My immortality carried a $10 price tag.

I'm not talking about the kind of immortality where you live forever and see miracles of the future, such as having diets banned by a constitutional amendment or being able to use charge cards on Mars.

I'm thinking in terms of having part of me last beyond the final date on my headstone.

Having a speeding ticket listed in the local newspaper and then knowing that the newspaper has been recorded on microfilm for posterity is one kind of immortality.

I've known women who have created wonderful recipes in their kitchens and those recipes are passed from one generation to another.

One weathered card in my recipe box is labelled "Aunt Marie's Chocolate Cake", and although I can't recall anyone with that name, part of her lives forever between a recipe for spinach salad and another for never-fail fudge.

Judging from the condition of the card, I suspect that Aunt Marie's recipe dates back to the time her husband was inventing the wheel.

I thought about receiving my immortality in the same way, but I seriously doubt that my recipe for baking frozen pizza will stand the test of time. Neither will my tuna fish casserole.

The recent publication of my book was accompanied by a blizzard of paperwork. I sent off for a Library of Congress number (so that librarians would know where to file my book), and an International Standard Book Number (so people in remote corners of the world would know where to order copies). I also applied for a copyright.

Like most other government forms, the application wanted to know everything, including my grandmother's favorite breakfast food and whether I would bear arms for my country in the event of war. I also sent along a check for $10, which I conscientiously avoided stapling, folding or mutilating.

The official copyright certificate arrived this week without much fanfare. I halfway expected a brass band after all of the paperwork, but it's merely a photocopy of my original application with a rather official looking stamp on the top. It's my key to immortality.

It means that the title and the book's words are protected for as long as I live plus 75 years. If someday, in the far-off future, a comedian on a space station uses any of the book's material, my great-grandchildren's attorneys will take the matter up with the party in question. My great-grandchildren will never have to worry about the price of chocolate again.

The notion of immortality won't help me much, but at least my descendents will be happy.

Melts in Your Helmet - Not on Your Hands

I have always considered chocolate to be the perfect food. I was wrong.

Responding to the hot temperatures of the Saudi Arabian desert (up to 120 degrees) and the fact that chocolate melts at 78 degrees, candy manufacturers in Hershey, PA, have risen to the challenge. They've invented a chocolate bar guaranteed to maintain its shape, without turning into a dripping mess, up to 100 degrees.

Since they have responded so well to one crisis I would like to suggest some additional changes for our domestic chocolate bars.

For one thing, they sould consider changing the packaging of candy bars. When I'm in a grocery store, surrounded by other shopping carts filled with granola, fresh vegetables and yogurt, it's easy to feel guilty about loading up my cart with frozen pizzas and candy bars.

Try as I might to tell onlookers about my rare chocolate deficiency, they only shake their heads in disbelief.

If those brilliant researchers could come up with creative packaging, I could make my chocolate pursases more discreetly. If chocolate bars could be concealed in heads of lettuce or made to look like bunches of celery, life in the check-out lane would be much less complicated.

They should also do something about the chocolate bars which leap, quite unnoticed, into the carts of unsuspecting shoppers.

It's possible for me to enter a grocery store with the sole intention of buying a can of floor wax, but when I return home, a handful of chocolate bars is found in the bottom of the bag. I honestly don't know how they get in there.

If it's happened once, it's happened a thousand times. I'll be walking through the store, pushing my cart as innocently as possible. Perhaps I'll buy a bag of onions and a few other items on my list. I resist temptation as I race my cart blindly down the candy aisle, trying my best to ignore the chocolate stars and the chocolate-peanut clusters.

But as the salesclerk rings up my sale, she'll ask, "Are all of these candy bars yours?" or "Did you have a coupon for this case of chocolate marshmallow Easter eggs?"

It's not what she says that's the most embarrassing, but rather the gasps of the customers standing behind me.

Instead of creating a scene and trying to explain how those items leaped into my cart when I wasn't looking, I make some unintelligible noises and pay for everything.

Yes, if the chocolate researchers could keep those candy bars from jumping into my cart when I don't want them, and at the same time develop some creative packaging for when I do, chocolate would be perfect.

Winter Thrills

I'm not much of an outdoor person during the winter.

While some people find dubious satisfaction in careening around the country on snowmobiles or risking life and limb on ski slopes, I prefer to hibernate. If Mother Nature had intended to have us go outside during the winter, we would have been born with thick coats of fur and feet shaped like snowshoes.

However, when I'm forced to face the elements, there are two activities guaranteed to give me an immediate rush of adrenaline: kicking snow chunks off cars and taking ditches.

Although kicking snow chunks runs a certain degree of risk, in the form of broken toes and scuffed boots, there's a lot to be said for redistributing large clumps of snow, ice and dirt from one part of the countryside to another. Listening to the splat of the chunk as it hits the pavement is probably one of the highlights of winter for me. I apparently have a low threshold for instant gratification.

As far as thrills go, kicking snow chunks ranks right up there with grabbing a shovel and knocking long icicles from the roof of a house.

Like many other people in the Upper Midwest, I also take ditches during the winter.

I've never heard a person say, "I really did a foolish thing today. I lost complete control of my car on the ice and landed up in a ditch."

Instead, they say "I took the ditch today" or "I headed for the ditch." To say anything else would imply an inability to cope with one's surroundings and a cowardly nature.

"Taking a ditch" sounds like a voluntary act, well

thought out and the only honorable thing to do, given the circumstances. In fact, when some people boast about taking a ditch it's as if it was on their list of things to do that day, along with shopping for groceries or showing up for a haircut.

One of my most memorable ditch leaps took place several years ago, one day after my husband and I returned from a winter escape to Hawaii. On my way to work in a neighboring town, I drove over a hill only to find the road completely blocked by a tow truck removing another car from the ditch.

My choices were few, given my inability to stop on the snow covered road. I could either hit the car, the truck or I could take the ditch. As my life flashed before my eyes, I wisely chose the latter course of action.

A farmer, who had been following me down the road, stopped his truck, got out and surveyed the damage.

As he walked around my car, which was lying spread-eagle in the ditch with snow up to its axles, he kicked one of the front tires and gave a low whistle.

"Will I be able to get it out?" I asked from the opened window.

"Depends," he answered, giving the front tire another kick. "Where did you get your tan?"

"Hawaii", I murmured into my coat collar. For a fleeting instant I was sure that I was about to be denied help on the grounds of having a tan out of season.

He gave a low "hrumph" and mumbled something into his collar. Luck was on my side and he pulled my car out of the ditch, anyway.

At work I talked about "taking the ditch", but I didn't mention, that in at least one man's eyes, I was a wimp for missing a few days of a Midwestern winter.

Attack of the Cash Machine

Bank cash cards are wonderful if you read the directions.

I used one for the first time this week and it was anything but the experience portrayed in the television commercials. Fortunately, no alarms went off and I didn't spend the night in jail.

We received the cash card, our passport to shopping convenience, when we opened a new checking account this year. Apparently, we should have opted for a less complicated toaster or a stadium blanket.

I decided to use the card when I found myself halfway through a Christmas list and the only items of value left in my billfold were a ball of lint and photos of my children. Although our children are definitely above average, I doubted whether their baby pictures could be passed off as currency.

"Let's try the cash card," I told my husband, who was already exhibiting the first danger signals of a shopping overdose.

After weaving up and down the halls of the crowded shopping mall, we finally located a cash machine. Any big game hunter would have admired our relentless search for the machine bearing the same logo as the one shown on my card.

In awe of the wonders of electronic banking, I followed the machine's direction, "INSERT CARD."

"This is going to be easy," I told my husband. I inserted the card and instead of spewing out money, the machine ordered, "PUNCH IN PERSONAL IDENTIFICATION NUMBER."

"What personal identification number?" I shouted at the machine. Not programmed for verbal attacks, the machine maintained a stony silence.

"I think it's the number I saw tucked in your billfold," murmured my husband from beneath his load of shopping bags.

As I rummaged through my billfold, dropping half of its contents on the floor, the machine began buzzing and flashing the words, "WAITING...WAITING".

The slip of paper with four numbers was finally located between a three-month photo of a toothless daughter and a grocery store coupon which expired three years ago.

The four numbers, which I had intended to memorize, were punched into the impatient machine.

"INVALID NUMBER," it bleeped. "PLEASE REPEAT PROCEDURE." In obvious contempt for human frailty, the machine spat out my card.

I meekly followed the directions. After all, I reasoned, if I have trouble remembering my children's names, it's very possible I punched the wrong numbers into the machine.

This time the machine became much more excited.

"INVALID ID NUMBER. CARD IS BEING RETAINED. PLEASE CONTACT YOUR BANK."

For all the machine knew, I was a purse snatcher, if not an escaped felon.

Now both cardless and moneyless, I knew that an embarrassing call would have to be made to our bank the next morning.

I also became painfully aware of another fact. The four numbers printed on the scrap of paper belonged to another credit card.

With buzzers sounding and lights flashing on the machine behind us, we left the mall through the nearest exit.

Free at Last

Sometimes they come back.

When our second daughter found out she was being transferred by her company to Sioux Falls, only 30 minutes away, she joined the countless stream of young people returning to their parents' homes.

Although I seriously doubt she is moving back in for our charming company and warmth, she managed to give us sound reasons for her return. The rent would be low, the food is good and she would no longer have to pay for cable TV.

One night last week, we returned home after an evening out and found her voice on our answering machine.

"Hi, Mom and Dad. I don't know where you are because you didn't tell me you were going away tonight." Her tone was accusatory and I suddenly identified with the hapless victims of the Inquisition. I feel compelled to make some response.

Things have changed around here since you baby birds fled the nest.

We no longer have to wait for people to shampoo, blow dry their hair and use a curling iron before we leave the house. Our departures are much more spontaneous. At the spur of the moment we might decide to go out and buy antacids or a loaf of bread. If you should return home from work and find an empty house, that means we're not home. We no longer do notes.

The menus have also changed considerably. After bowing to the food preferences of our children for almost 20 years, we're finally eating our favorite foods again - hot dogs and polish sausages. One of my friends, whose children have all left home, admitted that for 20 years she couldn't cook anything with tomatoes or onions. She now eats those foods to her heart's content.

Once we eat, however, the routine is fairly predictable. Your father has his chair and I have mine. You should feel free to use any leftover chair at the table. I no longer spend half the meal wiping up spilled milk and broken glass from the floor.

Remember those talks we used to have until the middle of the night? Now I usually fall asleep on the living room couch before the 10 o'clock news. Our idea of real excitement is making a batch of microwave popcorn and staying up for the weather forecast.

In spite of this, don't think for a moment that the intervening years have turned us into a boring, middle-aged couple. Sometimes we have dental appointments. At other times, we have hair cuts.

We've come a long way, baby.

Galileo - A Good Excuse not to Dust

The Thanksgiving leftovers may be still lingering, but it's already time to be thinking about baking, addressing Christmas cards and stringing outside lights on the house.

Are you bogged down with tings that have to be done before the holidays? Well, there's good news. The perfect excuse to put off those chores is on the way.

In fact, it's barreling toward the earth at 18,000 MPH and it goes by the name of Galileo.

The spacecraft was launched from Cape Canaveral last year and the National Aeronautics and Space Administration planned to have it swoop by Earth on December 8 so it could pick up speed from our gravity system and spin off toward Jupiter. It sounds very complicated and I must admit that 18,000 MPH is faster than I've ever driven.

It's predicted that Galileo will fly by our planet about 600 miles above sea level before it soars off into space. It's the "about" that makes me hesitant about tackling any holiday planning.

If a heavy payload headed directly for your living room doesn't make you think twice about giving up holiday chores, nothing will. I, for one, won't start looking for my recipe file until after 2:35 CST, December 8, when the spacecraft should be zipping over Miami.

I may not have a scientific background, but it seems that even a breadbox zoning in at 18,000 MPH could have a devastating effect on our home's general appearance.

"Look at this article," I told my husband. "It says that Galileo is loaded with scientific equipment and 50 pounds of platinum. Does this mean that with a direct hit, we could all become blondes?"

"That's plutonium," he corrected me as he scanned the article. "If anything would go wrong, you wouldn't have any hair to worry about."

Although NASA scientists don't foresee any problems, it's as good an excuse as any to put off what has to be done for the holidays until December 9.

Because procrastination seems to be my middle name, I won't have to look too far for other excuses. Unscheduled snowstorms and minor technicalities like broken fingernails and unfavorable horoscopes should keep me going until at least the end of the year.

When I serve our guests boxes of crackers instead of home baked delicacies and a carry-out pizza instead of a complete meal, I'll be sure to tell them about Galileo. I'm sure they will understand.

The Big City

After four years of college and three years of law school, our oldest daughter will soon decide where to live.

We never really expected her to move back to our hometown after seeing the bright lights of big cities. Once you've tasted sushi, gone to a movie theatre with at least a dozen screens and ridden in a taxi, any small town would seem pretty uneventful.

The good news is that one of her choices is Minneapolis, the geographical and moral equivalent of heaven. The bad news is that the other choice is Chicago, seven hours further away and once the home of Al Capone. Having our daughter live in Chicago isn't a pretty picture.

Although the choice she should make is perfectly clear to her father and me, we decided to sit on our hands and allow her to make the final decision. She is, after all, 25 years old, and she should be able to decide between Door One and Door Two.

On the outside chance that she couldn't decide between a smog-suffocating city, that in my mind has come to represent evil, and a lovely city boasting lakes, parks and trees, I called her on the phone. My intention was to broach the subject subtly.

"So - where are you going to live?" I blurted out when she answered the phone. Subtlety has never been one of my virtues. "For crying out loud, how could you ever consider living in Chicago?"

"Who is this?" she asked.

"It's your mother. You've probably forgotten what my voice sounds like. I just wanted you to know that it's all right if you want to live in Chicago."

I was on a roll, and my pledges to stay out of her

decision-making went the way of my other intentions to diet and return library books on time.

"It's all right you know. Oh, sure, you think you might move back to Minnesota someday, but you'll probably get married, buy a house, settle down and have children and we'll never see you again. But that's okay, too, because you'll be able to make video tapes of the children and when we watch them it will be just like being there.

"We'll ask perfect strangers to take our photos from time to time so you'll know how we have changed over the years.

"And what's the big fuss about Christmas? It's just another day.

"And we won't worry about you being mugged or being caught in the middle of some riot about garbage collection or some other crisis in the city. We won't worry at all."

At the end of my litany about the evils of Chicago, our daughter assured me that Minneapolis was still one of her favorite cities. As she talked I could hear sirens in the background.

Before we hung up, she promised to make a wise decision about her future.

In return, I promised to send her a can of Mace.

A mother can never be too careful.

The Dangers of Having a Pet

There's one more reason not to buy a pet.

About 50 snakes sold to a chain of New York City pet stores as harmless garter snakes turned out to be poisonous Asian water snakes. The mistake wasn't discovered until after some had been already sold to the public.

Most of my experiences with pets have been short-lived. We owned a bassett hound for one afternoon and one cat turned our home into a chamber of horrors for the better part of one year.

While we were still living in the country, Barney, the basset hound, was given to us by his city owners. We were told that Barney needed more space. Unknown to all parties involved, Barney was a cold-blooded killer.

For most of his first afternoon with us, Barney was content to lie on the middle of the living room floor where people could step over him. He did a fairly good imitation of a dead dog until we decided to let him outside while we went to town.

Barney seemed like a dream-come-true house pet. Because of his laid-back disposition it seemed unlikely that he would ever jump onto the furniture or ever move much faster than a snail. Thanks to Barney, our children would have lives much like Timmy and Tommy from the old Lassie TV series. If called upon, he would rescue them from abandoned wells and would know how to dial 911.

We weren't prepared for the grim battlefield that met us on our return from town. From one end of the yard to another, dead ducks were strewn all over. During one brief hour, our flock of 24 young ducks had become history.

We had no way of knowing that Barney had been

given small, stuffed animals while he was growing up in the city. Evidently, he took great delight in swinging the toys around by their necks between his many naps.

Because of his fowl behavior, Barney was immediately dispatched to a sheep ranch in South Dakota.

Tabatha, a Siamese cat with an attitude problem, was the next pet to join our family. Our home became her domain and while she became the darling of everyone else in our family, there was bad chemistry between the two of us.

When everyone else was off to work or school, our home became her battlefield and as I shuffled from one room to another, she would lie in waiting beneath beds and on top of cabinets.

I wasn't her favorite human, and she made it clear that she would like to see me banished, preferably to a sheep ranch in South Dakota.

Because I could never be sure when she would lunge for my ankles or some other sensitive part of my anatomy, I would approach each room in the house with caution and fear.

"Okay, cat, I'm going to make the bed now," I would call out. "Let's not have any trouble, okay?"

Unfortunately, trouble was her middle name.

While Tabatha had been declawed, we had overlooked the possibility of having her defanged, and she viewed me as some sort of walking smorgasbord. No bed could be made without some encounter with the attack cat.

After I issued an ultimatum, noting that either the cat or I would have to go, the family vote was close, 3-2. Tabatha, the guerrilla cat, was sent to another state.

Please don't misunderstand me. I know that there are millions of pet owners whose lives have been made richer by having animal companions. We simply had two unlucky experiences with the animal kingdom.

In fact, I'm surprised that one of those poisonous snakes didn't find its way into our lives.

The Working Mommy Doll

Move over, Barbie, and make way for the latest role model for little girls - the working mommy doll.

At first, it sounded like a good idea. However, the doll is unlike any working mother I've ever known.

Her accessories include a navy blue business suit, a briefcase, a baby, a baby carrier and a leisure outfit. The working mommy doll also has a perpetual smile on her face.

The fixed smile is the first giveaway that we're talking about some mythical mother. Show me a working mother who smiles constantly and I'll show you someone out of touch with reality. If the doll was realistic, it would grimace, groan, pout and sulk, at least occasionally.

I once bought a navy blue suit while our children were still young. The purchase was a flight into fantasy and it became a perfect catch-all for baby blanket lint, drool and burp marks. By the time I could safely wear the suit in public, it was hopelessly out of style.

"This doll is a reflection of our times," explained one of the two designers, both young mothers from New York.

Perhaps she could also explain the doll's leisure outfit. If a working mother can balance housework with a career and still find time for leisure, something has been overlooked. Either the mother in question stashes all of the dirty dishes in a closet or her children have nothing clean to wear to school.

I spend about 12 minutes a day with leisure activities like eating and brushing my teeth. By the time I would change into a leisure outfit, it would be time to take it off again.

Unless a true-to-life, working mommy doll comes around, little girls will be given unrealistic expectations, not unlike those given to us when we were influenced by Barbie dolls.

Unfortunately, very few of us grew up to have bouffant hairdos twice the width of our heads, tiny, little waistlines and pink convertibles.

When it came to realism, Barbie was a washout.

If I were to design a working mommy doll, based on real life, the accessories would be considerably different. They would include little pairs of pantyhose, complete with runs, aspirin and a tiny microwave oven for heating leftovers.

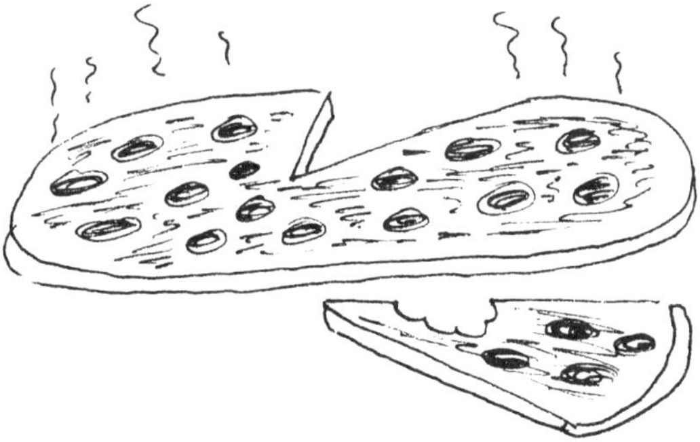

My version of the doll would also talk. It would say "Tonight we're having frozen pizza", "For this I went to college?", "I have better things to do than clean up after all of you", and the classic "I have a headache."

In order to be anatomically correct, my doll would also have stretch marks, funny little veins running down her legs and swollen feet.

It may not be the most attractive doll on the market, but it would truly be a reflection of our times.

No One's Perfect

The 10-year-old salesman and I were a winning combination.

He knocked on our door one evening this week, hoping to raise money for his hockey league. I had been sitting on the couch, fantasizing about chocolate and wishing that some would be dropped on my doorstep.

"Would you like to buy some chocolates?" he asked timidly. As a part of his sales pitch, he held out an assortment of chocolates. My trained eye immediately identified them as chocolate covered almonds, a chocolate bar and chocolate-mint meltaways.

Although my first instinct was to grab all of the chocolates and consume them as he stood there, I exercised admirable restraint.

"Would I?" I repeated cooly. The unsuspecting hocky player apparently had no idea he was dealing with a certified chocoholic. While he thought I was mulling over his sales technique, I was actually calculating how long it would take to pay for the chocolates, send the fledgling salesman on his way and have the chocolates to myself.

For all he knew, I purchased all three boxes out of sheer loyalty to the hockey league. The only thing that kept me from consuming all of the chocolates behind the closed front door was the knowledge that my husband had been listening to the entire transaction from his chair in the living room.

I can't eat unlimited quantities of chocolate with witnesses around. It's more of a private, religious experience. Eating chocolate in front of another person requires absolute restraint. It means taking dainty bites from one piece of chocolate and saying afterwards, "Wasn't that filling?"

Chocolate has never been a synonym for moderation.

So he and I split the chocolate bar and I reluctantly placed the two boxes of chocolate high on a kitchen shelf.

I didn't think about them again until the following afternoon when I returned home from teaching.

My original intent had been to eat only one of the chocolate covered almonds and then return the carefully resealed box to the shelf. No one would notice if one tiny piece of candy was missing. Within seconds, I had removed a few more pieces.

My trips to the cupboard became more frequent and less covert. I tried shuffling the contents of the box around in order to make it appear still full. Before I realized what had happened, there were only two pieces left.

I was then faced with an ethical decision. Should I leave the nearly empty box on the shelf for my husband to find, or should I destroy the evidence completely and hope that he had forgotten there were two boxes on the shelf?

I chose the latter course of action and hoped that he would be none the wiser.

When he returned home from work, one hour after the first piece of chocolate had been so cleverly removed from the box, I tried my best to conceal my tell-tale chocolate breath. It was the closest I've ever come to an Academy Award-winning performance.

He put his arm around my shoulder and exclaimed, "You know, I'm very proud of you. I came home this noon and there were still two boxes of chocolates in the cupboard."

His praise caught me off guard. As I blurted out the truth about the chocolates and confessed my activities for the past hour, he looked as though someone had slapped him across the face.

Actually, it was a good experience for both of us. I had my fill of chocolate and he finally discovered I wasn't perfect.

Christmas Letters

It's a novel idea.

My brainstorm came after reading about the California woman who writes personalized novels, complete with the names of real people. Using a computer to insert the couple's names and details from their personal lives into steamy novels, she has already cranked out at least 1,500 copies at $150 each.

What we could really use is a personalized Christmas letter, ready to be photocopied. The good news is that it's free. All you have to do is underline the correct completions and fill in the blanks.

HOLIDAY GREETINGS
FROM THE____________

Please forgive us for sending a form letter, but we've been busy this year remodeling our home. This year we added (a swimming pool) (two bedrooms and a hot tub) (new maid's quarters).

____________(Husband's name) was especially excited about seeing the project completed after he (won the Pulitzer Prize for literature) (won the Minnesota lottery) (was featured on the cover of *Time*).

Although____________(wife's name) has (gone back to school and earned her PhD in biophysics in one amazing summer session) (canned 150 quarts of tomatoes from her garden) (been jogging 10 miles a day) she doesn't look a day over (30) (30) (30).

Our son, ____________, graduated summa cum

laude from (Yale) (Harvard) (Princeton) this spring. During his senior year, he (accidentally discovered the cure for the common cold while working on a term paper) (won the Heisman Trophy) (was asked to fill in when the university president took an early retirement).

Our daughter, ____________, is a ravishing beauty and is often mistaken for (Madonna) (Molly Ringwald) (Debra Winger). On a whim this year, she entered the Miss ____________(your state) contest and won by a landslide.

We knew ____________(daughter's name) had won the contest when she told the emcee, "I would like to see a better world for future generations and peace everywhere." After her reign, she hopes to become (an interpreter for the U.N.) (a figure-skater in the next Winter Olympics) (a U.S. senator).

Our (dog) (cat) (parakeet) was neutered this summer and the entire experience was totally exhausting for all of us, so we spent a relaxing month in (Tahiti) (Paris) (Monacco). Buying a new (BMW) (Mercedes) (Ferrari) also helped lift our spirits.

Please let us hear from you soon. Merry Christmas.

The Greasy Look

Dirty, greasy-looking hair is "in".

Although the news comes too late to prevent our family from investing a small fortune in hair products, it should be good news for families with teenagers.

According to an article in the *Wall Street Journal*, trend setters are going as long as two weeks between shampoos. A Swedish hairdresser, who served as the inspiration for the new look, hasn't washed his hair in seven years.

An L.A. hairdresser noted, "It does look a bit weighted down, but it looks okay - a lot of people don't like really clean hair."

While all of our daughters were home, shampoos and showers were daily rituals, followed religiously. The only thing that would have kept them from washing their hair daily would have been the well going dry, or some other natural disaster.

They would have rather kissed their parents in public or worn the same prom dress twice than go without shampooing. Our meals and routines revolved around their shampoo schedules.

We bought hair products in such large quantities that the major manufacturers of shampoos and conditioners no doubt referred to our family by name at their sales meetings. I wouldn't have been surprised if they would have invited us to their office Christmas parties.

The article also noted that American consumers

spent $2.2 billion in shampoos and conditioners last year. That's not at all surprising. We must have spent at least half that amount while the girls were still home.

Another interesting fact: Our country apparently has more blow-dryers than any other nation. If that doesn't make you swell with pride, nothing will.

When our older girls left for college, they took along a disproportionate amount of blow-dryers and hair curlers. In fact, when they moved all of their hair appliances from home to other parts of the state, the earth's axis shifted by a few degrees.

One day I explained to my daughters how we only used to take baths on Saturday nights when we were young and how we went for days without shampooing. Judging from the shocked expressions on their faces, it was a miracle we had survived such deprivation. I didn't bother to explain that my brothers, sisters and I used to share the same bath water in order to conserve hot water. They didn't seem ready for the harsher realities of life.

Spokesmen for the new dirty hair look note that greasy products are available for those who refuse to stop shampooing their hair, but want to look disheveled anyway.

That way, it's possible to look "in" without risking mites, itchy scalp and smelling like yesterday's socks.

The Shot

It wasn't the shot heard 'round the world, but I certainly stood up and took notice.

Recently I came down with an insufferable cold -insufferable for my family to be more exact. Like most mothers I rarely find the time to be sick, but when I do manage to catch a bug, everyone around me lies low until the white flag appears.

By the second week of my most recent cold, our older daughters had stopped calling home to check on my health and my husband was showing the first warning signs of a frozen pizza overdose.

For almost two weeks, I did a fairly remarkable imitation of Elizabeth Barrett Browning, who was never a picture of health. I swooned, coughed and ran up the stock of most tissue companies. It was a cold to end all colds.

My husband, by then well past his fifth meal of take-home broasted chicken and macaroni salads from the deli, finally suggested that I call the doctor and make an appointment.

"It's only a cold," I told the receptionist on the phone. "You won't have to weigh me."

The fear of having my weight recorded by complete strangers is about the only thing that keeps me from visiting the doctor more often. Actually, the medical center is a pleasant place to visit. There's always someone to talk with and they have a wide variety of magazines.

By the time I saw the doctor the cold had spread to most parts of my body and I looked like a poster child for the bubonic plague.

After listening to my chest and checking my pulse for vital signs, he recommended a shot of penicillin. Wishing me a speedy recovery and writing out a prescription for other antibiotics, he noted the nurse would give me the shot.

Left alone in the room, I decided that the shot would no doubt be administered to my left arm. I rolled up my sleeve and waited patiently for the nurse's entrance.

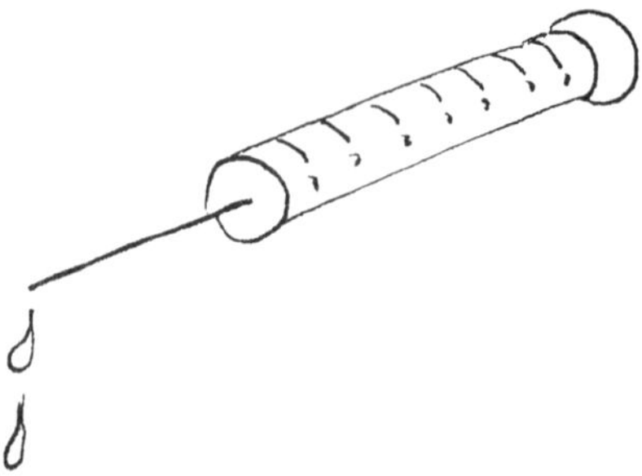

However, she had different ideas.

Armed with an ear-to-ear smile and a syringe at least a foot long, she advised me, "Bend over and pull down your slacks. This shouldn't hurt."

Quite suddenly I recalled the second reason why my visits to the doctor are so infrequent. I have real reservations about baring my largest muscle when there are witnesses around.

The memory of that shot returned vividly today when I read about a California hospital that's offering free drive-through flu shots to motorists. In its news release the Pomona Valley Hospital Medical Center advised, "Roll up your sleeve and put your arm out the car window."

Obviously, some members of the medical community have decided to ride the wake left by fast food restaurants.

As Thanksgiving approaches, I am especially grateful that our medical center wasn't using the drive-in approach when I had to bare it all.

The Milkman Cometh

He was the other man in my mother's life.

One of my earliest memories includes the screeching of brakes in our driveway as the milkman made one of his predawn stops at our house. He ignored the normal sleep patterns of the rest of the world as he walked to our back door with the wire basket of glass bottles clanging against his legs.

For those of us who wanted to sleep until a more civilized hour, the milkman became one of life's necessary evils. If I would complain about the noise the milkman created, my mother would handle my grievances in a rational manner.

"If the milkman stops coming here," she advised, "all of your teeth will fall out." There was no arguing with logic.

I never saw the milkman -only the notes my mother would leave for him.

"Leave 2 homog" was her most frequent message, usually written on any available scrap of paper she was able to salvage. Before special holidays she would become more literary.

"Need 3 homog, 1 whp cr and 1 sr cr" she would write. Mother was a woman of few words and they were all cryptic.

The tradition of having a milkman continued for 10 years after my husband and I were married. Milk was no longer delivered in glass bottles, but rather in cardboard cartons. Unlike the faceless, nameless milk carriers of my childhood, our milkmen only worked during daylight hours.

For 10 luxurious, calcium-filled years, I never met a milkman I didn't like. They were always pleasant and willing to pass the time of day, discussing politics, the weather, road conditions and the price of milk. While our children were young, the milkman was my primary link with the outside world.

Suddenly, they were gone. They vanished from the face of the earth, along with telephone operators and the men who used to wash our car windows in gas stations.

According to a recent magazine article, milkmen are staging a comeback. The Palm Beach Milk Co. opened in May and expects to have 1500 route customers by this fall. Another company in New Jersey estimates that about 25 percent of its business comes from home delivery. Both companies are delivering milk in reusable glass bottles.

We should also expect to see a revival of milkman stories. After we had a brunette daughter, following the births of two blondes, I often explained that we had switched milkmen. It was much more fun than explaining the basic facts of gene pools.

I had no idea our third daughter would take the story seriously.

A few years later, while she and I were shopping, we ran across our displaced milkman, now working in a store.

Several customers were standing behind us at the counter when I chose to introduce her to Harold (not his real name).

"You remember Harold, don't you?" I asked her.

"Of course," she exclaimed. "You're my father!" There were audible gasps from the line behind us.

It suddenly became quite clear why milkmen had willingly chosen other lines of work. The stories and gasps got to them.

The Raccoon War

Our lake home has a wonderful view, filled with flora and fauna. Last week I declared open war on the fauna.

I really didn't have any other course to take. All I know is that my recent experiences would turn the most zealous, animal rights activist into an avid hunter.

The large raccoon who has been ransacking our garbage pails on a nightly basis is no longer concerned with his basic rights. What he wants is complete dominion of the world.

Deep down, I know the raccoon is only doing what comes naturally. He's foraging for food, taking care of his young and laughing behind my back. In the process, he's turning our entire lawn into a compost pile of egg shells, coffee grounds and leftovers from forgettable meals.

I can never forgive him for that.

We purchased two plastic garbage cans with snap-on lids in a futile attempt to thwart his midnight raids. When the raccoon figured out that the garbage could be reached by knocking the cans over and springing the lids, we went one step further.

We pounded heavy steel stakes into the ground and tied the cans to them with heavy-duty nylon rope, capable of towing a large ship into harbor. During the first night with the stakes and ropes, the ropes were shredded while we slept, and garbage was strewn all over our lawn.

I began going to bed later and getting up earlier, hoping to catch the dastardly fiend in his tracks. As I became a victim of sleep deprivation, I could only conclude that the raccoon struck somewhere between midnight and 5 a.m.

Heavy anchors were placed on the tops of the

cans, but that tactic was also unsuccessful. My mind began wandering to thoughts of hand grenades and bazookas.

Last night, as I was just falling asleep, I heard the thunk-a-thunk of garbage cans shaking against the house. With bare feet and wearing only my nightie, I leaped around the corner of the house and confronted the raccoon.

He was the biggest raccoon I've ever seen. He must have weighed as much as one of my thighs, and he threw me a look that snorted, "Go ahead, lady, make my day!"

As the masked intruder sat on his throne of torn plastic bags and munched merrily away on a wilted celery stalk, he refused to budge, no matter how much I jumped up and down and hurled insults at him.

I grabbed the nearby garden hose and turned on the faucet, hoping to send him scurrying. As the water sprayed in his face, he didn't blink an eye, but rather, kept gnawing away at the celery.

It was the great standoff of all times. He sat there, holding his spoils of war, and I stood only a few feet away, with the water hose dripping down my arm and creating a mud puddle under my feet.

At last, the moment of truth came.

"All right!" I screamed. "Have it your way!" I stormed into the house and later dreamed about raccoons and heavy artillery.

The Golf Tournament

Being an athlete is much more difficult than it appears.

Before entering a golf tournament last summer, I had never been in any athletic competition. I had never experienced the sweetness of victory or the bitterness of defeat.

While I was in high school, the athletic girls could only become pom-pom girls and cheerleaders. The rest of us joined the Spanish Club. On a scale of athletic prowess, I have always ranked somewhere between a clam and a sea sponge.

Without knowing the difference between a tournament flight and a handicap, I entered the tournament with high hopes. While listening to the news one day, I happened to hear the scores from a professional golf tour and I was surprised to hear the winning scores in the 60s and 70s.

Since my golf scores were dipping down to the low 50s, I figured that I was ready for the big time. Not one of the sports announcers bothered to mention that they were talking about 18 holes, not nine.

When I showed up at the golf course for the first day of match play, I was psychologically prepared. I was wearing my lucky shoes, my lucky socks and my lucky shorts. As I stood on the first tee and chatted amiably with my opponent, I gave serious thought to where the tournament trophy would be placed on our fireplace mantel.

The first round of the tournament was a dismal failure. My opponent, who clearly was a professional playing under an assumed name, drove her ball straight down the fairways. As I took the more scenic route, through trees, under shrubs and down ditches, it soon became apparent that my lucky outfit wasn't going to do the trick.

On the second day, I showed up for consolation play. It would be my last chance to redeem myself. I teed off first and as the ball landed just short of the green, my opponent was the first to speak.

"You know, I play mostly for the fun of it," she smiled. "I don't play to win."

That was good news. Since she was playing for fun and I was playing for blood, we seemed like the ideal twosome. I wondered whether the consolation trophy would look best on the dining room table or on one of my book shelves.

It was a tight game. At the end of our round, she had won three holes, I had won three and we were tied on the other three.

The winner would be determined with the 10th hole - the sudden death, the final test, the moment of truth.

We both landed on the final green with three strokes each. While her ball rested at least 12 feet from the cup, and mine was only three feet from imminent victory, I imagined what it would be like to cradle the trophy in my hands and I mentally wrote out my acceptance speech.

My dreams were dashed as she lined up the ball and took a lethal swing. Her ball plunked into the cup.

That was it. All I had to do was sink the ball and the game would once more be tied. I took careful aim and let the club kiss the side of the ball. As the ball rolled interminably toward the hole, the world seemed frozen in suspended animation.

The ball died one foot short of the hole.

Although the return trip to the clubhouse is

blurred in my memory, I do remember congratulating my opponent and someone else saying, "Better luck next year."

At least I learned a valuable lesson that day. When people say, "I don't play to win, I play for the fun of it," what they actually mean is "Get out of my way- that trophy has my name on it."

Up, Up and a Weigh

An airplane trip doesn't have to be a guilt trip.

Passengers should be able to savor flying above the clouds, looking at in-flight magazines and sipping complimentary beverages served in plastic glasses. Flying should be an enjoyable experience.

What a person weighs shouldn't be a problem.

Recently, for the second time in my life, my weight was taken into consideration before a plane could leave the ground.

Several years ago, my husband and I boarded a plane scheduled to fly from the Hawaiian island, Molokai, to Maui. As we prepared to walk out to the island hopper, we were stopped by a flight attendant carrying a clipboard.

"Excuse me," she blurted, "but could you please give me your weights?"

"Why do you want to know?" I answered, rather defensively.

She explained that the plane was about to take off from a very short runway that ended rather abruptly at the edge of a steep cliff. The total weight of the passengers would determine whether or not the plane would plummet into the Pacific Ocean far beneath us.

In my mind, it was a flimsy excuse. For all I knew, she was an informant for my doctor.

"I weigh 100," I responded without batting an eye. Two could play that game. It was none of her business that I had more likely consumed that number of pounds in pineapple that morning.

I did experience a few qualms as the plane barreled down the runway, but apparently other passengers said they weighed more than they actually did. Things have a way of working out.

Last week, the same husband and I boarded a

shuttle flight from Minneapolis to Worthington, MN. It was a small, no-frills plane and we hadn't been assigned seats.

I had just wedged my knees behind the pilot's seat when an airline employee came aboard the plane with a clipboard. Seeing her gave me an eeire sense of deja vu.

"You will all have to sit in assigned seats," she informed up. "The weight has to be evenly distributed."

I took the news personally and tried my best to look small.

Because the plane's interior was roughly the size of your average bathroom, we all had to get off the plane first. For one brief moment, it appeared that the pilot's plastic seat, which had become fused to my kneecaps, was going to leave the plane with me.

There was considerable mumbling and grumbling on the ground as we waited for our new seat numbers to be called. Then I decided to be quiet.

Once we were in our new seats, it was very unsettling to discover that I was seated opposite a man who could have been a sumo wrestler. I tried sucking in my cheeks in a feeble effort to look gaunt, but the airline employee seemed satisfied with the new arrangement.

Quite miraculously, the plane didn't flip over in mid-flight and we landed safely.

From now on, I will only fly in large planes, where one's weight isn't a matter of life and death.

Fashion Magazine Models

Fall fashion catalogs have been bombarding our home on a daily basis.

Because I'm reluctant to throw them away, our living room resembles the reading room at the public library. The magazine rack is filled to overflowing and every table top is covered with the promises of instant glamor in exchange for my credit card number and a completed order form.

One of the leisure wear catalogs features long-legged, willowy models standing in the middle of wheat fields or on the edges of windswept cliffs. They try to look as relaxed as possible in $200 sweaters and skirts. Personally, I would be afraid to move - not because of the cliffs, but because of the price tags.

Photos of models doing real weekend activities, like carrying out the trash, cleaning out the garage and washing clothes, are conspicuously missing.

As they stand in the wheat fields, wearing high fashion boots, long, swirling skirts, slouchy hats and baggy sweaters, the models look gaunt and hungry. The unwritten message is that I could look the same way.

In real life, if I wore the same outfit in a nearby farm field, I would probably be picked up for vagrancy.

There are photos of attractive young men and women attending polo matches, just standing around or wandering aimlessly through woods. With distant looks in their eyes, they appear to be lost or looking for a fast food restaurant.

"We'll fit you beautifully" claims another catalog, specializing in styles for hard-to-fit women. According to their size charts on the back page, hard-to-fit includes any woman wearing a size 12 or larger. Roughly translated, it means most of us - normal women.

The catalog obviously doesn't subscribe to the prinicples of truth in advertising because all of the models have protruding hipbones and cheekbones. They have evidently never chomped into a cream-filled eclair or eaten half of a large pizza.

Covered with needless yards of extra fabric, they smile brightly from the catalog pages, and their message is clear: Buy this outfit and you, too, will look thin and emaciated.

I could possibly achieve the same effect by draping myself in a circus tent.

It would be much more honest to have regular sized women, complete with wrinkles and bulges, modeling the fashions in the hard-to-fit catalog.

Forget the polo fields and the models who probably can't remember which year they had their last meal.

Show me an honest catalog, depicting real people doing real activities, and I'll show you a happy shopper.

The High School Reunion (Part One)

The road to a high school class reunion is paved with good intentions.

After the invitation to my 30th reunion arrived a few months ago, I immediately composed a list of things to do before the big day.

In all of the excitement, I was bound to forget something.

The last time I saw those classmates, Fidel Castro was still our hero. My girlfriends wore crinolines and the boys drove Nash Ramblers.

Before I would be able to greet them on a first name basis, I needed a crash course in recall. It seemed like an insurmountable task - I can't remember the first names of our children most of the time.

I hoped that my high school yearbook would jar loose a few memories. The book was finally located on a top book shelf between some cobweb-covered cookbooks and a neatly bound packet of Christmas cards that were never mailed out in 1972.

Several hours were spent looking at photos of 418 classmates I should have known. There were boys with flattop haircuts and girls wearing sweaters and strings of pearls. Many of the pages were covered with farewell inscriptions written by Jackie, Loie, Nancy, Jerry and many others.

I couldn't be sure, but they sounded vaguely like the names of Mouseketeers. Whoever they were, they all wrote with common themes: good luck in the future, and never forget the good times we had in (study hall, 7th hour English, journalism class). Whatever the message, it was clear that 1960 was pretty much the end of the world.

There was something else I wanted to do, but I couldn't remember.

Before I could attend the reunion, I also needed something to wear. My first instinct was to wear a poodle skirt for old times' sake, but if any of my classmates belong to the National Society for the Prevention of Cruelty to Animals, they wouldn't be amused.

I finally settled on a comfortable, blousy dress which makes me look like one of the robust wheat gatherers in Millet's "The Gleaners". If anyone laughs, I simply won't invite them to my next slumber party.

For all they know, every Minnesota woman dresses that way. There's a certain geographical advantage in living far away from one's hometown.

I've never attended a class reunion, but I assume the 30th should be fairly safe. It's hard to imagine any 48-year-old woman without her fair share of stretch marks, liver spots, legs that look like highway maps or bifocals. Either that, or I'm headed for the biggest disappointment in my life.

I tried without success to remember what else I wanted to do. Today, four days before our departure, it hit me like the proverbial ton of bricks.

I had intended to lose 20 pounds, but I forgot.

The High School Reunion (Part Two)

There's bad news, fellow potato chip lovers. The clothing designers have turned on us again.

The hot new look in summer dresses, according to Catherine Cook of the *Baltimore Sun*, is "a clingy little slip of a dress that shows off lots of cleavage and plenty of leg."

"In general," the article continued, "necklines are lower than ever and hemlines higher than in previous seasons."

That's all fine and dandy, but I happen to lack the one necessary requirement for the new, little dress: a little body.

I went shopping recently for a summer dress to wear to my upcoming 30th high school reunion, and I was dismayed to see so little material sold for so much money. At least packing for the reunion would be simplified, because I would be able to carry quite a few dresses in my purse.

"I want something that makes me look like a perky cheerleader from the 50s," I told the salesclerk. I didn't bother to explain that I had never been one because jumping around a football field would have kept me too far from the concession stands.

"How about something in raw silk?" she asked. "It's quite the rage this year."

After trying on the dress, I could better understand what she meant by "rage." Thousands of hard-working silkworms would have become outraged if they could have seen me.

After trying on her second selection, a hot neon orange dress, complete with horizontal stripes, I resembled one of the warning barrels set out on the center lines during highway construction projects.

The only accessories needed to make the look complete would have been a flagman and a hard hat.

Undaunted in my pursuit of the perfect dress, I spied a flowered print among the single-digit sizes. Realizing that the tiny dress would only cover one of my thighs, I asked to see the same size dress in my size.

It too was a disappointment. While the dress on the rack was two flowers wide, my version looked like an entire garden. I hadn't seen so many flowers since my last visit to a greenhouse. Rather than looking like a successful high school graduate, I looked like a garden fertilizer ad.

The only way I'll be able to look like the classmate they all remember at the reunion is to show up wearing a loose-fitting graduation gown or my favorite bathrobe.

The High School Reunion (Part Three)

At first it seemed like one, huge mistake.

What should have been my 1960 high school class reunion looked like a meeting of senior citizens. My first impression was that my husband and I had shown up at the wrong restaurant.

The reunion was well underway by the time we found it near the shore of Lake Michigan, and the crowd was a rolling sea of bald heads, gray hair and complete strangers peering down their noses through bifocals.

After poring through the pages of my high school annual for two weeks, trying to remember faces and names of friends I promised never to forget, I had felt well prepared.

I knew that I had changed. You can't spend 30 years eating chocolate, ordering carry-out pizza and raising a family and expect to look like Miss America. After looking at their faded photos in the annual, I remembered my classmates as they once were.

They would still look like football players, cheerleaders and members of the band and the speech team.

I was a stranger, trapped in a time warp. Instead of finding football jerseys and red and white pom-poms, there were these old people, sharing photos of grandchildren and apparently having the time of their lives.

I watched and listened carefully as they stood around us, hoping to find a familiar face. Suddenly there was a woman's scream behind me.

"Rissy!"

My old nickname triggered a happy medley of memories: standing in the school hallway between clases, sharing a double chocolate malt, made with real ice cream, with a friend, listening to Frankie Avalon croon over the Wurlitzer, smelling tanning oils on the beach during summer vacations and admiring boys' class rings wrapped with tape.

It had to be Karen, and I turned around to face one of my best friends from high school. In one split second, I realized that she had also been ordering carry-out pizzas and eating chocolates for the better part of three decades. Hugging her seemed very natural and it was like hugging the past.

Between the two of us, we recognized a pair of eyes there and a smile here. Most of the voices hadn't changed.

The evening flew by and each minute held a new discovery. For five exciting hours I was flung back through time to a world where there were no tranisitor radios, personal computers or S and L debts. Vietnam was only a dot on the map and having clear skin and a date for Saturday night were the most important things in the world.

It was also interesting to find out where our paths had led. One friend, a cheerleader, managed to cheer her way through college and she continues to be a cheerleading advisor in a small high school. Another friend, who our teachers were convinced would someday land up in the state prison making license plates, became a high school principal.

Perhaps the greatest discovery was that you can go home again. Faces and bodies may change, but if you squint your eyes, you might catch a glimpse of yesterday.

The Senseless Robbery

I've had a nice, symbiotic relationship with a candy store all summer.

Goodies, a handmade candy shop in Arnolds Park, IA, has become one of my main reasons for living.

They specialize in hand-dipped, creamy chocolate truffles and every week I gladly exchange my pay check for an ample supply of their caramel turtles and countless pounds of chocolate delicacies.

In the general scheme of things, truffles have become as important to me as manna was to the Israelites or ambrosia was to the Greek and Roman gods.

Rather appropriately, biting into a truffle can be a meaningful, religious experience.

Our interdependent relationship was seriously threatened two weeks ago when my favorite store was robbed at gunpoint.

Until the unwitting robbers decided foolishly to take the store's money and leave the priceless truffles behind, the store and I had a smooth working relationship.

I would give them all of my available cash and they would use the money to buy more slabs of chocolate and other necessary ingredients to make more candy for me to buy the following week. It was a happy cycle.

Robbing the store was an odious, senseless crime. It ranks right up there with robbing a church poor box or stealing candy from babies.

Taking the money from the register and leaving the truffles behind is comparable to breaking into the Louvre and overlooking the Mona Lisa. It's like robbing the pop machines at Fort Knox and leaving the gold behind.

Not only have the unknown robbers broken several state and federal laws, they have also made laughingstocks of themselves among chocolate connoisseurs. Many of us consider chocolate to be a basic food group. Eating chocolate is not a privilege, but rather an undeniable right.

When they're finally apprehended and sent up the river, how will they explain their crime to their cell mates?

It would be difficult to stand up to a mountain of a man, named "Killer" and wearing a tattoo showing a skull and crossbones and the word "Mother", and tell him the truth.

It would be especially difficult if Killer was also a confirmed chocoholic and had no sense of humor.

The candy store robbers have given all criminals a bad name. Is nothing sacred anymore?

How Far is 100 Miles?

Last year, 375 runners and walkers participated in the 14th Annual Western States 100-Mile Endurance Race.

Their happy feet took them from Lake Tahoe to Auburn, CA. I'm only surprised they didn't learn their lesson the first year.

I can't imagine running or walking for 100 miles. For that matter, I can't even imagine driving in a car for that distance. A car trip alone would require two rest room stops and four stops at fast food restaurants.

The magazine article describing the race tried to explain how far 100 miles would be. It noted that 100 miles would be the equivalent of climbing up and down the stairs of Chicago's 110-story Sears Tower 364 times, or taking 952 trips to the top of the Washington Monument in Washington, DC.

Since I've never been to those places, and I would surmise that others haven't either, I would like to explain the distance of 100 miles in everyday terms.

That's roughly the distance from the street to the front foor of the dentist's office when you've been scheduled for extensive dental work and you know that you have a low pain threshold.

One hundred miles is the distance you have to walk from the shopping mall to your car. It seems at least that long after you've sworn on a stack of credit cards to everyone with you that finding the car will be no problem. On the third or fourth trip around the entire mall, even loyal children can become openly hostile.

It takes at least 100 miles of walking to find the items on your shopping list at the grocery store after the store manager has completely rearranged the shelves. It's very disconcerting to reach for a box of corn flakes and come up with a bunch of broccoli.

One hundred miles is the distance you have to walk to be introduced to the woman wearing the same dress you're wearing at a party. It's also the same distance you try to keep between the dresses after you discover hers is a size four and yours is a size 14. It's a small consolation to realize that you received more fabric for the money.

When the needle on your car's gas gauge is below the red danger mark and you've assured everyone in the car that there's plenty of gas left in the tank, the closest gas station will be 100 miles down the road.

On the other hand, I would gladly walk 100 miles for a hot fudge sundae. It's all relative.

Easy Rider

It's true. Once you've learned how to ride a bike, you never forget.

One day this week, while the family car was tied up, I needed to pick up some clothing at the dry cleaner's.

I could have walked, but I decided instead to ride the bicycle left behind by a daughter who discovered driving a car is more fun.

The bike looked different from the bike I rode some 30-odd years ago. The tires were skinnier and the seat looked perfect for someone with 20-inch hips.

The first couple blocks of my journey were relatively uneventful. A few tourists gasped with awe before they took my photos and cars swerved to avoid hitting me.

As I soared toward the first stop sign, I discovered another major difference between this bike and the one I rode during grade school: this one had hand brakes. The brakes were applied only microseconds before I would have seriously disrupted the normal flow of traffic on Main Street and made front page headlines.

However, the stop was so sudden that I nearly flew over the handlebars like a stone released from a slingshot. My entire life flashed before my eyes and I was suddenly very sorry I had never traveled to Europe.

My heart began beating normally by the time I reached the dry cleaner's. As I climbed back onto the bike, I draped the dry cleaning over my back with my left hand and securely wrapped the strap to my shoulder purse around my neck. Without a basket on the bike, it appeared to be the only way to travel.

As I headed home, it became clear that the garment hangers would cut through my fingers, or I would become strangled by my own credit cards, long before I would see my kitchen again.

There was also the matter of the hill. In a car, it had always seemed like a slight incline, but on a bike it resembled an Alpine slope. Houses flew past and small children ran for their mothers' sides as I flew like an eagle down the sloping street with the dry cleaning and my purse flapping wildly behind me.

After some fumbling with the right hand brake, it suddenly occurred to me that both brakes would have to be activated to make the bike stop. Instead of lunging into the busy intersection by our house, I chose a precarious course of action.

Like a bicycle version of Mario Andretti, I cut into a neighbor's driveway close to the corner and peeled over his neatly manicured lawn in an attempt to slow down the bike. It worked. Instead of approaching our own driveway at the speed of sound, I must have decreased my speed to 30 or 40 MPH.

Although jumping isn't one of my main strengths, I jumped off the bike and somehow managed to keep my pride intact. My fingers had become numbed under the pressure of the hangers and the purse strap had virtually cut off the circulation from my brain to the rest of my body, but I was alive.

I would have kissed the ground if the school playground across the street hadn't been filled with curious, open-mouthed children.

In another 30 years, I might try riding a bike again.

My Memories of Chubby Checker

My life has been a long series of near misses.

Except for a narrow margin of 1,000 votes, I could have been homecoming queen at my high school.

When word leaked out that my children existed solely on frozen pizzas and macaroni and cheese, I lost my chance at being named Mother of the Year in 1983.

I missed receiving a Phi Beta Kappa key by a few miserable grade points.

Chubby Checker has now been added to my list of near misses. When I woke up one Friday morning, this summer, I was confident that my interview with him would be a sure thing. Within six hours, my chances were about as sure as having an entire summer without television re-runs.

At the prospect of meeting one of my top three teenage idols, with Annette Funicello and "Wild Kingdom's" Marlin Perkins being the other two, I had done careful research on the 19-year-old former chicken plucker who had twisted his way into my adolescent heart.

On the morning of the interview I put on pantyhose, a feat normally reserved for summer weddings and funerals. I also wore a dress, an act so unusual that, had she know about it, would have thrown my mother into cardiac arrest.

I didn't dare use the phone, out of fear I would miss the phone call from the amusement park where he was scheduled to appear that night. I read and reread my research notes as I sat by the phone and waited for my rendezvous with destiny.

By noon my appearance had begun to wilt. I had eaten three boxes of crackers and I had called AT&T at least a dozen times to determine whether phones were no longer operable in the Upper Midwest.

By midafternoon, my pantyhose had become permanently fused to my legs in the sultry heat, and I thought about Larry, the creep who had stood me up for the junior prom in high school. In my mind, Larry assumed the face of Chubby Checker, who had been born Ernest Evans in Philadelphia in October, 1941. One of my fondest dreams has been to drive over Larry with a car someday.

As the stifling, afternoon sun made the day less and less tolerable and my patience reached the point of no-return, I gave new meaning to the expression, "Hell knows no fury like a woman scorned." As I began hallucinating, Larry-Chubby became my Nemesis.

During a relatively brief period of clear thought, I called the park and asked the woman who answered, "Is Chubby there?"

"He's resting now," she told me. "He's very tired."

"Well," I blurted out, "I wouldn't go to the prom with him if he was the last man on earth!" I slammed down the phone receiver in desperation.

Because of Chubby Checker, I have sworn off chicken. It's the only logical thing to do.

I will most certainly never twist again, like I did last summer.

The Old Bachelor

The old bachelor is gone. Actually, I'm not sure if he ever married, how or if he celebrated his birthdays or what his life was like.

I passed his house every time I drove from our lake home to Spirit Lake. Almost hidden behind an overgrown stand of lilac bushes, the small house hadn't aged well. Scabby flecks of white paint were barely visible on the weathered wood, and the house looked as if it was being swallowed alive by the undisciplined grass and weeds.

He would stand like a silent sentinel by the edge of the road, watching the traffic go by. If I would give him a country salute, by lifting my index finger from its grip on the top of the steering wheel, he would always smile and wave back. He was a lean, unshaven man who wore shapeless bib overalls.

A rusty sign, on what must have once been a front lawn, appeared to be standing on its toes to see over the runaway grass. I slowed down one day to read the sign, when the bachelor wasn't in sight, and the faded letters read "This is a completely electric home."

As I glanced up at the derelict house, it was difficult to imagine a time when someone must have been proud to live there. When the sign was put up, were there clothesline crisp curtains in the windows? Did peony bushes bloom there in the early summer?

Sometimes I look at older people and imagine what they looked like when they were young. For several summers, I did the same thing with the weather flogged house and its arm-waving occupant.

Because I didn't know him, I could only imagine his life story.

John Doe was the brain child of the Iowa Department of Tourism. He was hired, at considerable cost to the state, to stand by the side of the road and wave at passing tourists with their campers and boat trailers. Hired to perpetuate the myth of rustic, rural living, John Doe became himself only when he entered the aging farm house. He actually held a Ph.D. in sociology from the University of Iowa.

Each evening, as he exchanged his bib overalls for a polo shirt, designer slacks and comfortable deck shoes, he would listen to classical music from public radio.

The refrigerator and kitchen shelves held his favorite foods, including tofu, alfalfa sprouts and granola. The state-of-the-art kitchen, complete with a food processor and a microwave oven, was adjacent to the living room, resplendent with its highly buffed, blond oak floor, indirect lighting and modular furniture.

Book shelves, holding the works of every author on the best-seller lists and art books from the world's foremost art museums, lined one wall of the living room. Except for a scattering of original Picassos, the stark white walls throughout the house gave it a sense of spaciousness. Potted plants, including a lush fig tree and a thick palm, added vitality to the rooms.

The bedroom was highlighted by a water bed, covered neatly with black satin sheets, and exercise equipment.

The old bachelor is gone this summer. The vintage car is no longer in sight and the driveway has been choked by grass and a fallen tree branch.

Perhaps the state withdrew its local color appropriation and the old bachelor moved down to the

Florida Keys, where he works as an Ernest Hemingway lookalike.

I miss his smile and wave.

Doilies

Doilies are making a comeback.

Fashion forecasters are saying lace is the look for the kinder, gentler '90s, but I am sure they have never lived with the horror of doilies.

While I was growing up, grandmothers used to crochet doilies featuring elaborate pineapple designs. I'm not sure, but I think it was part of their job description.

After the doilies were stiffly starched and pressed for endless hours, they were given away as gifts for most of the major holidays, bridal showers and weddings. Once they worked their way into our homes, they were draped over the backs and arms of living room chairs and sofas.

My mother wasn't an exception when it came to decorating every surface in the living room with doilies. As children, we were constantly admonished to not mess up the doilies. It seemed like an insurmountable task because the doilies slid like melted butter off the furniture, which was covered with protective, clear plastic slipcovers.

The plastic covers on the furniture complemented the protective cellophane wrappings left on the lamp shades. My mother's moral commitment to keeping furniture in its factory condition was further evidenced by her unwillingness to cut "Do Not Remove this Tag Under Penalty of Law" labels from chair cushions and mattresses.

My mother seemed obligated to keep each piece of furniture in showroom condition until we all left home. Her worst scenario in life would have been to walk into the living room and discover a peanut butter sandwich smeared into the nylon upholstery.

In a moment of desperation, my mother one day decided to fasten the doilies to the slipcovers with carefully concealed straight pins. As a result, every member of my family had pierced elbows and necks, long before pierced ears became the rage.

Sitting down to relax and having a straight pin jammed two inches into your forearm is not unlike acupuncture. Both experiences tend to make you forget all of your other problems and allow you to concentrate on the immediate pain. At least acupuncture provides some sort of warning before contact is established.

Based on my old puncture marks, I can honestly state there's nothing kind or gentle about having doilies in the house.

Postage Stamps take a Licking

It sounds like one of those good news-bad news stories.

The bad news is that on March 6, 1990, the U.S. Postal Service will consider increasing the cost of mailing a first-class letter to 30 cents.

The good news is that they hope to have only one other increase before the end of this century.

The 20 percent increase, the largest ever, would take effect next February.

If this rate of inflation keeps up, it may be possible to spend more on stamps for paying our bills than we spend on the bills themselves.

There may come a day, heaven forbid, when we have to walk downtown and pay the bills in person. The postage increase might actually be part of a devious government plot to keep us physically fit.

Some of us will think twice before using a 30-cent stamp to send for a company's 25-cent refund. Unless we will miss our pen pal relationships with post office boxes in White Plains, NY, and Little America, MN, it just won't be worthwhile to squeeze our names and addresses onto those tiny refund forms any longer.

When you think about it, the end of the century isn't all that far off. If another 20 percent increase should occur before then, it may be necessary to take out a loan before sending off our Christmas cards.

I guess it all boils down to the quality of postal service we would like to receive. Is it worth it to have someone trudge to our front doors, through rain, snow, sleet and hail, for 30 cents?

It's not as though we have another postal service at our disposal, either. What we have is what we get.

Without money to pay for expenses, the postal service might have to make some drastic cuts. It might mean having our mail thrown onto our front lawns two days a week or going without colorful commemorative stamps.

The worst scenario would have the mail truck dropping off large canvas bags of mail in some central part of town, such as the elementary playground or the city park. It would be up to volunteers to sort out the mail. There would be no secrets as friends and neighbors would rifle through our bank overdrafts, overdue library notices and other mail.

I have a still better solution. Why not charge first class postage for all of the junk mail we receive daily? Why should a distributor of pantyhose get a better price break than the rest of us?

The positive effects of such a plan could be twofold. There would be less junk mail and there would be more income for the postal service.

It won't work, though. It's too practical.

The Leisure Life of Lobsters

I wouldn't mind changing places with a lobster on a cold winter day.

Millions of jet-set lobsters are flown from Maine to Asia every year, and now their shippers are planning stopovers for the lobsters in Hawaii. The surfside accomodations are needed because the lobsters suffer from jet lag on non-stop flights.

Jet lag is fatal for a fourth of the lobsters. It's not a case of disoriented lobsters asking each other, "What day is this?" or "What's the time?" They don't wonder if it's time for breakfast or dinner. They simply go claws up.

Before you begin feeling sorry for the little crustaceans, ask yourself a few questions. When was the last time someone offered to fly you to the Orient and pay you $40 a pound? When was the last time you flew anywhere with a stopover in Hawaii?

At $40 a pound I could afford to fly to the moon and back and still have enough change left over for postcards.

Stopovers in Hawaii will allow for the tired lobsters to stretch their claws and absorb oxygen from Pacific seawater before resuming their trip.

Granted, the end of a trip for a lobster might mean being thrown into a pot of boiling water, but that's how most people feel when they return to work after a vacation.

People manage to get into plenty of hot water without the benefit of a plane trip halfway around the world.

If it would be possible to stretch out on a tropical beach and soak in Pacific oxygen for an extended period of time, I would be willing to suffer almost any consequence. It wouldn't be too thrilling to become the main course for a meal, such as Columnist Thermidor, but I'm sure arrangements could be worked out once I got there.

Shippers, rather than animal activists, are behind the plans for lobster stopovers in Hawaii.

At this time of year, most of us could use people activists. Our activists would boldly ask, "What are these people doing in this intolerable weather? Let's send them to a warmer climate!"

People should receive at least half the consideration shown to lobsters.

The next time you're shoveling the driveway or thawing out your fingers, try not to think about the vacationing lobsters.

Why I Gain Weight During the Winter

The average person gains seven and a half pounds during the winter.

The reasons for these weight gains are fairly obvious to most of us. There are few interesting things to do outside in the winter without the risk of having frostbitten appendages or falling asleep in a snowbank and never waking up.

Winter is a grim season, and for that reason, most of us prefer to stay inside. My favorite indoor activity is the care and maintenance of kitchen appliances.

If it were not for keeping the appliances in perfect working order, the national weight gain average might have been held down to six pounds. By keeping an eagle eye on my refrigerator, microwave and stove I more than made up for the people who didn't gain weight this winter.

My fetish with kitchen appliances is a matter of choice. Should I carry in a cord of firewood from the backyard or should I eat half a cake? Should I chop the ice on the driveway or should I bake a batch of brownies?

Several hours each winter are set aside to check if the refrigerator light is still working. If you check the refrigerator light enough times, it's also possible to work on a healthy tan.

Since the refrigerator door has to be opened to check on the light anyway, why not sample a dish or two from the shelves to make sure the temperature controls are working? For best results, a random sampling should be made of most of the refrigerator's contents.

It's a small price to pay to avoid giving an entire family a good case of food poisoning.

The microwave oven should also be checked frequently. As anyone knows, a microwave should not be run when it's empty. In order to test the microwave's efficiency, it might be necessary to make a cup of hot chocolate. A dollop of whipping cream from the refrigerator would take care of two appliances at the same time.

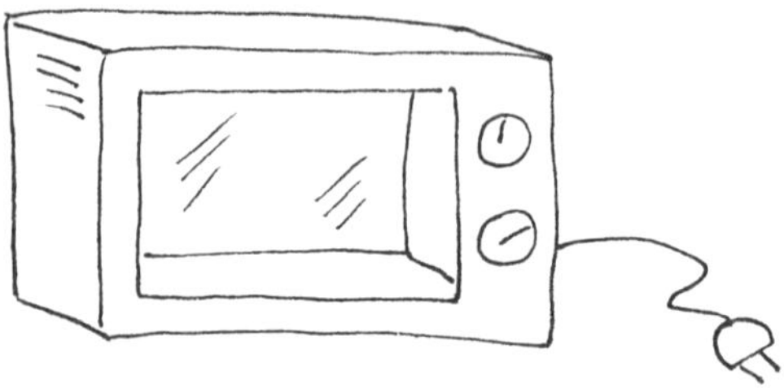

And what better way is there to check the working order of an oven than to throw in a test bundt cake? By actually baking something, it's possible to check the oven coils and see if the stove has been properly balanced. If the cake appears to be uneven on top, readjust the stove legs and try baking something else. Don't stop this pattern until the stove is in tiptop condition.

Keeping kitchen appliances in perfect working order is a responsibility none of us should ignore.

Show me a person who didn't gain weight this winter, and I'll show you a kitchen full of neglected appliances.

On Being Dutch

I can't imagine being too Dutchy.

It's much like having someone criticize the way you breathe or the way your fingernails grow. When it came to nationality, I can't recall being given a wide variety of choices.

In a recent newspaper article, it was revealed that actress Loretta Young's real name was Gretchen Michaela Young. The article went on to explain, "Studio officials suggested she change it because Gretchen sounded too Dutchy."

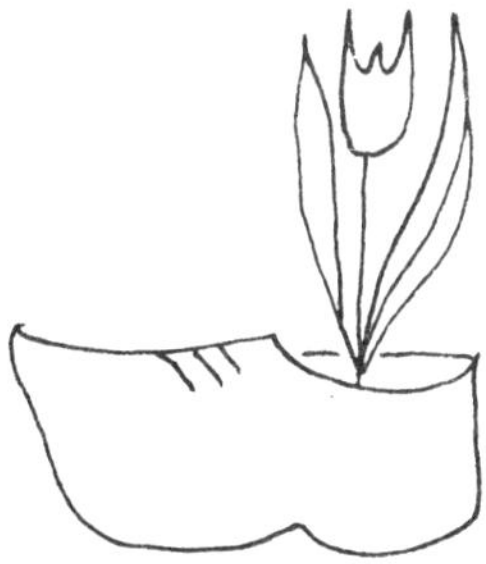

I was brought up in a predominatly Dutch community, Holland, Michigan. One of my father's favorite quotes was "If you're not Dutch, you're not much." Of course, he was the same person who told me, "If you cross your eyes, they will stay that way" and "If you climb that tree, you'll break your leg." One out of three isn't all that bad.

Now that the stigma of having a Dutch name has been made painfully clear, the setbacks in my life finally have been explained.

I now understand why I was never chosen as homecoming queen when I was in high school. For years I figured it had something to do with my figure or my personality. It was the name and nothing else.

I've never won a door prize at a Tuppeware party. I have never been considered as a likely candidate for Mrs. America. Life would have been considerably different with a name like Smith or Jones.

Although we didn't realize that our names would hinder us later in life, my classmates and I were instilled with a strong sense of pride in our national heritage. Without the Dutch, we knew, the world would be tulipless and edam cheeseless, and the art world would have missed Van Gogh and Rembrandt.

We immortalized Albertus C. Van Raalte, who founded our town in 1847, when he and his followers decided to escape religious persecution in their homeland. However, Albertus was not without his faults.

After a church organ had been dismantled in the old country, it was transported by sea and land to the fledgling community on a journey which took the better part of a year.

After he heard a local woman, no doubt one of my rebellious ancestors, play non-religious music on the organ, Albertus had the organ destroyed. It was taken out into the town square, where it was axed to pieces and burned.

Fires played an important role in my hometown's colorful history. At the same time as the Chicago fire, 1871, my hometown also burned down completely. For a long time the founding fathers debated whether sparks from Chicago had traveled over Lake Michigan and started the fire, or if it had been the wrath of God, punishing them for unmentionable sins.

For all I know, the debate is still raging in my hometown, which must be the only place in the country that levies a stiff fine for picking tulips.

I may be held back because of my name, but I certainly have a nice background in the finer points of punishment.

The Shrinker Strikes Again

It's much easier to camoflage a few extra pounds during the winter.

Goose down jackets are great equalizers, giving everyone the appearance of a walking marshmallow. Once we have been covered from head to toe with protective winter covering, we all resemble finalists in a Nanook of the North look-alike contest.

Summer is a different story when the all-revealing bathing suits and shorts make their appearances. After the bathing suits are taken out of storage and tried on for the first time, we are immediately divided into two distinct groups: the devil-may-care pizza eaters and the sullen celery eaters.

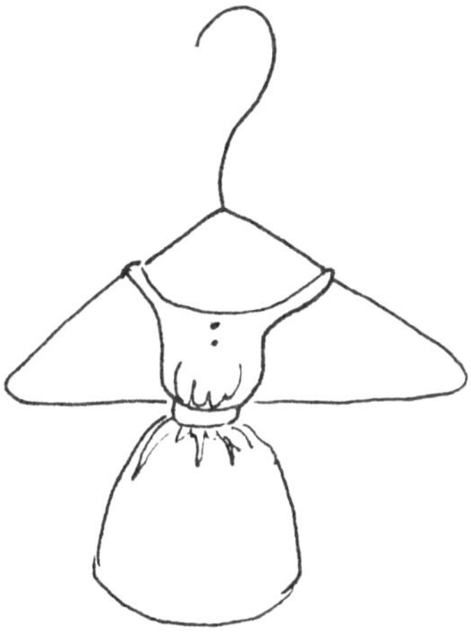

My bathing suit from last summer was a little, hot pink number and I fully expected it to fit again this year. I had no idea that putting it on for the first time would be like squeezing a 30-pound watermelon into one of those tiny, plastic sandwich bags. Spandex may be a wonderful fabric but it can't be expected to perform miracles and cover a multitude of eating sins.

There are plenty of good reasons why people have trouble fitting into last summer's swimwear. In his recent book, "On an Average Day...", author Tom Heymann reveals that on any given day Americans eat 2,739,726 Dunkin' Donuts and spend $3,561,644 on tortilla chips. We spend $21,917,808 on snack food a day.

While those might be good excuses for other people, I blame my ill-fitting suit on the Shrinker, an elusive culprit who invades our home each winter and reduces my clothing to Barbie doll size. It's the only sound explanation because I religiously follow a stringent physical fitness program all winter.

Instead of being carried to the refrigerator during television commercials, I always insist on walking there myself. Whenever I spread cheese on crackers, I use full arm movements. I open those vacuum sealed potato chips bags without any assistance. It's a tough regimen.

In spite of these good intentions to keep myself physically fit, the Shrinker has selected my wardrobe for his wrongdoings.

While I am gone for the day, he gathers up my shorts and bathing suits from the closet and runs them through my washing machine on the hot water cycle. When the articles of clothing meet his satisfaction and have been shrunk to half their normal size, he puts them in my clothes dryer where they are exposed to temperatures not unlike those found on the surface of the sun. Just before my clothes reach the melting point, they are carefully folded and returned to the closet.

On the fateful day last week when I tried on my bathing suit, I decided to sashay into the living room and see my husband's reaction.

To be quite honest, as I struggled to breathe in what should have been a lovely vision of hot pink, I felt as though I had just gone through a trash compacter. The Shrinker had certainly gone all out in his efforts this year.

My husband was at first speechless. His eyes reflected a combination of wonder and terror. He finally gasped, "Carole...is...that...you?"

I didn't bother to tell him about the Shrinker. Only another woman wedged into a bathing suit would understand.

Reverse Psychology

They apparently don't know about reverse psychology in Cincinnati.

A large group of indignant Cincinnatians had a good-sized tizzy-fit when photographer Robert Mapplethorpe's exhibit came to town last year. No parent who knows his or her beans would be surprised with the results.

While previous exhibits at the art gallery attracted 556 and 225 patrons daily, the controversial Mapplethorpe photograpy is drawing over 2,500 viewers a day. Surprise. Surprise.

It doesn't take a genius to figure out what happened in Cincinnati. If you tell people that something is bad for them, they will try to corner the market.

There's a good chance that if the President's mother would have admonished, "Don't eat the broccoli, George, it's bad for you", the vegetable would still be served aboard Air Force One.

My husband and I became introduced to the intricacies of reverse psychology shortly after our first daughter came home from the hospital. We had our agenda; she had hers.

Although we carefully explained to her the hours she should follow for eating, sleeping and burping, she belonged to another time zone. Chaos ruled our home until we figured out that "good for you" and "bad for you" should be switched around.

Simply saying something is "good for you" is like giving it the kiss of death. Show me a person who was told as a child, "Don't eat so much candy or all of your teeth will fall out" and I'll show you dental bills the size of the national defense budget.

When the same daughter grew older and began buying her own clothes, she came home one day with a new coat. When she modeled it for her father, he hedged the issue and asked, "Isn't that an awkward length?" From that moment on, she began wearing the coat 24 hours a day.

Two daughters later, we perfected reverse psychology to a fine art. Although we never had sons, we hope to have some voice in the selection of our future sons-in-law. After all, these are the people with whom we will be spending the rest of our holidays.

When the right ones come along we will only have to say, "This guy is an insult to humanity. He must never darken our doorstep again." All we will have to do after that is order the flowers, reserve the church and start making ham sandwiches.

By saying "What a nice young man! He reminds me of your father", I have already sentenced several hapless victims to a life of painful solitude and bachelorhood. In my book, those two terms are synonymous.

If the protesters in Cincinnati would have issued invitations to the photography exhibit, instead of creating such a fuss, things might have been different.

Dancing on the Height-Weight Tables

My level of happiness is directly related to recommended height-weight tables.

Happiness became downright jubilation last week when a revised table of recommended weights was released by two government agencies. In my opinion, the folks at the U.S. Department of Agriculture and the Department of Health and Human Services should be canonized for sainthood.

According to the new table, I could weigh anything between 144 and 183. I haven't felt so liberated since garter belts went out of style or "permanent press" became household words.

The bad news is that the new weight table doesn't count if your hip-waist ratio isn't right. Unless you've received a Ph.D. in mathematics and understand ratios, your correct weight is still anyone's guess.

A tape measure should be used to compare the hips and the waist. If your belly is close in size to your hips, or even larger, it's implied by the new table that you should be selecting your favorite hymns and the speaker for your eulogy.

Because I don't have a tape measure, it was difficult to determine my exact ratio. I vaguely recalled that a tape measure had something to do with sewing.

I gave up sewing about the same time an easy-to-sew dress pattern sent me over the brink of sanity.

The tape collected dust on a closet shelf until 1974 when it was cut into pieces and was used to tie tomato plants to their stakes.

Instead of a tape measure, I resorted to the next best thing - my husband's steel measuring tape.

As I stood in the kitchen and tried to wrap the

clumsy steel tape around my waist, I discovered that steel tapes don't go around a human form. Instead, they form sharp corners and kinks around anything within reach.

Cannisters were knocked helter-skelter and dishes fell off the counter as I wrestled with the tape and tried to determine my waist-hips ratio.

After several unsuccessful attempts, I could only conclude that my hips, the toaster and two kitchen chairs had a total circumference of 12 feet.

Totally exhausted, I didn't bother measuring my waist. I just assumed that it hadn't changed much since sixth grade.

According to the new charts, I don't have anything to worry about. With 12-foot hips and a 19-inch waist, I'm not fat.

I always knew the right chart would come along someday.

Sensitivity

I missed being a baby-boomer by four years.

That's my main excuse for not understanding ABC-TV's "Thirtysomething". After watching the program for the past season, trying to catch its substance, I continue to come up with fluff.

I have never seen so many characters speak so much about so little. PMS, sensitivity and mood swings seem to be the predominant themes of the show, although I might be missing the good stuff when I head for the refrigerator during commercials.

I've tried to imagine what life would be like with similar scripts.

"Hi, dear, I'm home!" my husband would call from the front door.

"Don't talk to me! Can't you see I'm upset? My kitchen wax is yellowing!"

"I understand. I care. Do you want to talk about it? I really do care, you know."

"All I know is that I was walking into the kitchen and they were there! Yellow spots all over!"

"Perhaps you should call an analyst. Talk it out with someone. I care, you know."

"I'm really down. All I know is that all day I've been thinking about the rain forests, the greenhouse effect, the ozone layer and my hair's split ends. It's been a terrible day. I saw the yellow spots on the floor and my whole world fell apart."

"It's good we can talk this way. I care, you know."

"And do you know what I saw in the full-length mirror this morning? More cellulite! I can't take this anymore! I'd like a divorce."

"Why don't you just calm down a little, dear? I'll make you a nice cup of herbal tea, give you a little space and perhaps you can get back in touch with your feelings."

After a few more "I care's" and the usual number of commercials, advising us to feed our dogs the proper diets based on their ages and to get rid of the ugly water spots on our stemware, this could be a complete script. All that would be needed to fill in the hour would be a few meaningful shoulder shrugs and some soul-searching music.

Actually, I'm glad that I was born in 1942 and that my own parents weren't acting like baby boomers during November, 1941.

"Dear, I was thinking. Wouldn't it be wonderful to have a baby girl? We could call her Carole. What do you think? I really care about your feelings."

"Oh, I don't think so. What with these terrible wars breaking out all over the world, do you really think this is a good time to have a baby? Let's have a cup of herbal tea instead and talk about it for the next hour."

I'm grateful that my parents decided to have me instead of a tea break.

The Garden is Still in the Store

We only wanted a simple vegetable garden. We hadn't intended to push a salesclerk over the edge of sanity in the process.

The time was right for a garden. The ducks and geese were flying north and my husband and I had already dog-eared the pages of seed catalogs for several months. We were anxious to work the rich loam soil of the garden with our hands and communicate with Mother Earth.

If the salesclerk could have communicated in the same way with her cash register, our dream garden would now be a reality.

My husband and I shared visions of a lush, green garden overflowing with succulent tomatoes and other produce. Once the ground had been reawakened with a tiller, we set off for town to purchase garden seeds.

Our first stop had a "Buy two packets, get one packet free" sale. With high hopes for a bountiful harvest, we selected countless packets of seeds. Green beans, carrots, spaghetti squash and a multitude of other vegetables would soon reign supreme in our little corner of the world.

In less time than it would take to say "hoe, hoe, hoe", the clerk quickly rang up the sale on the cash register and it appeared that the cost of the seeds would run close to the national debt. When my husband reminded her about the sale price, she became obviously perplexed. There were too many packets and too many different prices. The woman fell apart.

What should have been a simple task turned out to be an insurmountable problem for the salesclerk. She sighed, shuffled the packets on the counter and gave another sigh. We could have more easily asked her to explain the theory of relativity or how to conugate a series of Latin verbs.

In a way, the high technology of her electronic cash register was to blame. For too long she had simply rung up sales and had been told how much change to return to the customer. She hadn't been programmed to count seed packets and allow for discounts.

After several minutes of awkward silence, we realized that those hand-selected seeds would never reach our garden. An early clue was when the sales clerk began mumbling incoherently to herself as she shuffled the packets around in reckless abandon. The packets appeared and disappeared like so many tarot cards and, from where we were standing, the future looked bleak.

We left the store without making a purchase. For all we know, the salesclerk is still standing there, trying to make sense out of what should have been our garden.

Sometimes They Come Back

Being a parent has its fair share of worries.

While our children were still young, we worried about them scratching their chicken pox and whether they would get across streets safely. We worried about them falling out of trees or eating too much candy and having their teeth fall out.

We worried about sending them off to summer camps and later to college. We worried when they left the house and when they returned home.

Parents are designed to worry. That's why we come equipped with furrowed brows, sweat glands and front porch lights.

Like thousands of other college seniors across the country, our second daughter has become another cause for worry. Armed with college degrees in anthropology, psychology, medieval arts and other studies, the graduates are sending off their resumes in quest of the great American dream.

We aren't worried about whether she will graduate, but we do worry about whether she will find the ideal job. Forget ideal - let's just make it a job.

For all of those graduating seniors there is at least the same number of parents facing the biggest worry of all: WHAT IF THEY MOVE BACK HOME?

It should be written somewhere that once you leave home, you never move back.

The statistics say it all. Increasing numbers of young people between the ages of 19 and 24, whether they have jobs or not, are choosing to move back home with their parents. Living home with mom and dad is much less expensive than renting an apartment, buying groceries and making trips to a laundromat. It's more like winning a dream vacation.

Having a grown child move back home could have its drawbacks. For one thing, I doubt whether they would take kindly to being sent to their rooms or being grounded for keeping late hours. It would eliminate most of the excitement of being a parent.

Our home would be no exception. Since our two oldest daughters left for college, we have adjusted to a routine lifestyle. We sit at certain places at the table and we have our designated chairs in the living room. We eat at certain times and life has become reassuringly predictable.

Without the patter of little feet, life has become as comfortable as an old pair of socks.

Moving back to a house where you can only sit in certain chairs and only crunch loud carrot sticks during commercials would be a hardship for any persons in their right minds.

Don't misunderstand. We love to have them come home for visits and we enjoy keeping up with their lives. But somewhere along the way, while they were registering for college classes and adjusting to life elsewhere, we changed.

Thomas Wolfe once wrote "You can't go home again." You can go home again, but your parents won't be the same.

No Deposits, Please

Picky, picky, picky. That description fit the Citizens Bank in Weston, W.Va., when it refused to do any more business with a farmer who tracked dirt onto their newly installed carpet.

The farmer's account of $1,335.29 was closed after he left a trail of mud on the carpet for the second time in one week.

If we would have followed that same hard-lined policy years ago, while our children were still small, their first trips outdoors would have been their last. We would have lost them as companions and tax deductions while they were still toddlers.

It's too bad the bank never thought of the solution we hit upon when we were installing new carpeting a few years ago. We were living on a farm, and at least three tons of unsightly topsoil had accumulated on the living room and kitchen floors. Our daughters' shoes had some sort of magnetic attraction for driveway dirt.

I waged an all-out war on the tracked-in grit. I pleaded, cajoled, had them remove their shoes at the door and even considered awarding clean shoe awards. Nothing seemed to work. Cleaning the kitchen floor required a shovel and I was giving serious thought to buying a bulldozer.

If my idea catches on, carpet installers may soon be adding geologists to their crews.

One day I brought home several carpet samples from town. They were all shades of brown, and we scattered them like fallen leaves on the farm driveway. I was determined to find the perfect match.

One sample blended in perfectly with its surroundings. It was the color of the driveway with a slight hint of crankcase sludge. Once the carpeting was installed throughout the house, I never had to worry about unsightly spots again.

The floor still felt crunchy beneath our feet, but the difference in color was no longer noticeable.

My only other alternative would have been to follow the example set by my mother when all of her children finally left home. She had white carpeting installed in her living room and then cordoned off the entire room with velvet theatre roping. No one dared step into the room so the carpet stayed snow white for years.

If the bank in West Virginia would have taken the time to match their new carpeting with the topsoil in their area, they could have focused on the cash deposits in their bank, rather than the deposits on their carpeting.

A Cast for Thousands

Wait a minute. You haven't heard of everything until you've heard about the latest craze for expectant parents.

A Los Angeles couple has introduced a kit that allows a woman to make a plaster cast of her pregnant belly. The kit is quite complete. It includes plaster, gauze, two markers for friends' autographs and pink and blue ribbons for hanging the keepsake.

My darkest hour occurred when I was expecting our third daughter and my waist measured 54 inches. Of course, we didn't know it was a daughter at the time. From all appearances, it looked as though I was smuggling watermelons. Our second daughter had great hopes that our large bundle of joy would turn out to be a horse.

There are certain times in our lives that shouldn't be remembered and the final months of a pregnancy rank right up there. All I can recall is looking like the Goodyear blimp, not being able to see my feet and having people point at me when I waddled down the street.

The newspaper article didn't mention the cost of the kit, but there must be some proud parents out there who are willing to pay top dollar for a plaster cast of mommy's tummy.

All I know is that my wide expanse would have required enough plaster to cover the walls of a three-bedroom rambler. I would have needed enough gauze to keep a small hospital well supplied for a year.

Besides serving as a conversation piece on a living room wall, perhaps the plaster cast could also have some practical purposes.

It would make a spectacular salad bowl for large

dinner parties. It would also hold enough popcorn for a family of 12.

Other children in the family could share in the excitement of a pending birth by using the plaster cast as a snow coaster. They could also paint circles on the cast and use it as a three-dimensional dart board. It's possible that the plaster cast could provide a special bonding between an unborn baby and its siblings.

We've come a long way since a pending birth in a family was talked about in hushed tones and we vaguely referred to our mothers' "delicate conditions." We no longer refer to a woman as being "in the family way."

The only thing that could be in the family's way these days would be a 200-pound plaster cast of a large belly hanging on a living room wall.

The Dangers of Licking Toads

A lobbyist friend once told me, "There are two things people should never see: sausage being made and the state legislature while it's in session."

I wonder what he would say about the legislatures in Georgia and South Carolina. Both states introduced bills last year that would outlaw licking toads.

The Drug Enforcement Administration noted that certain toads secrete a hallucinogenic toxin.

It may soon be illegal for women to kiss an unspecified number of toads before they find a handsome prince.

With this new information, it's very possible that the childhood favorite, "The Frog Prince", will have to be rewritten. There's a good chance that when the princess discovered the prince in the guise of a frog, it wasn't really love. She heard fireworks because she was hallucinating.

What troubles me more than having a favorite fairy tale blown out of the water is wondering who took the time to lick a toad in the first place.

Did the person experiment with other rocks, plants and animals before licking the first toad, or was it a one time event?

Maybe it was one of those youngsters who put everything in their mouths, including pennies, marbles and toads.

"Put down that toad," his mother no doubt reprimanded him, "and wash your hands before supper."

No one suspected the harmful effects of the toad-licking until a few minutes later, when the small tyke began arguing with the mashed potatoes on his plate.

Perhaps it was a simple college fraternity prank.

"Hey, Joe, let's see you lick that toad!"

Some people will do anything on a dare and the fraternity brother was no exception. After his first close encounter with the toxic toad, he very likely gave it his fraternity pin and they lived happily forever on their own golden pond.

It wouldn't take a law to keep me from kissing, licking or even touching a toad. I would rather have root canal surgery without an anesthetic or walk barefoot through a bed of hot coals then have any type of relationship with a toad.

After a fair share of toads early in my life, I happily discovered my handsome prince 30 years ago. Until we finally croak, we'll just keep on hallucinating with each other and humming our favorite song.

Curious? It's "Have I Toad You Lately that I Love You?"

Driving Skills

Drivers training didn't prepare me for the real world.

Between teaching us how to change tires, which I have successfully avoided, and how to tell a piston from a fly wheel, the teacher should have told us something about defensive driving.

He should have mentioned the drivers who slow down to 20 MPH for stop signs, look both ways and keep on going. He should have talked about interstate driving, where passing drivers pull in front of you, leaving about three inches of breathing space between bumpers.

It would have helped if he would have mentioned tailgaters, the scourge of our highways. What's truly frightening about tailgaters is when I can read the headlines of their newspapers in my rear-view mirror.

While other drivers eat their meals, shave and use their telephones while operating their cars, it's downright challenging for the rest of us to get from one place to another.

To meet these needs, advanced driving schools are cropping up all over the country. One school in Georgia offers courses in everything from racing to chauffeur/counter terrorist driving.

Although it might not fit into their description of terrorists, I can't think of anything more terrifying than having tailgaters who are devouring four-course meals from a fast-food restaurant or combing their hair. I, for one, would hate to have my cause of death listed as a large order of fries.

A two-day racing course in Colorado offers a novice racing license and fireproof underwear. No kidding. Some of the schools are very practical.

I don't mean to imply that I'm a perfect driver. A

couple years ago, in downtown St. Paul, I rear-ended another car while I was touching up my lipstick. As a result of that mishap, I landed up with streak of bright-red lipstick across one entire side of my face and the lipstick tube stuck in my left ear. It was hardly a fashion statement as I bore a strong resemblance to Clarabelle the Clown.

My driving skills have improved considerably since the lipstick incident. As a matter of fact, several drivers have taken the time to signal their approval as I expertly weave in and out of the traffic.

At least I think they're showing their approval. They slam on their brakes, shake their fists and shout out compliments I can't quite hear.

People respect a good driver.

Cloth Diapers or Paper Diapers?

I didn't think I would ever say this, but there are certain advantages to being my age. I can remember changing cloth diapers.

Throwaway diapers have been receiving considerable amounts of bad press lately. People who are genuinely concerned with the environment would like to see them eliminated. The paper diapers, which I personally consider to be the ninth wonder of the world, are supposedly clogging up the nation's landfills and are a threat to future generations.

It's my contention that if we go back to cloth diapers, there will be no future generations anyway. Without access to paper diapers, having a baby would lose much of its charm and excitement.

I can remember back 25 years when soiled diapers had to be hand-dipped in toilets and wrung out with bare hands. An accomplished mother might be able to flush the toilet and hand-dip the diaper at the same time, but many of us were dismal failures. I lost my grip on more diapers to city sewer systems than I care to remember.

Wringing out a dirtied diaper with bare hands ranks right up there with wading barefoot through a cattle feedlot during a muddy spring or having an entire family come down with the stomach flu.

It's not a pretty picture.

Although I might be risking an unfair generalization, I wager that few of those anti-paper diaper activists have ever actually changed a cloth diaper. Twenty-five years ago it was a dubious privilege shared only by mothers and helpful grandmothers. They were the same raised voices who shouted their chorus of hallelujahs when paper diapers were invented.

If state legislatures decide to ban paper diapers, we might witness a general uproarious rebellion among fathers, daycare centers, babysitters and other first-timers to the world of cloth diapers. They will finally understand why past generations of mothers share two common traits, permanently wrinkled noses and a general distrust of strained prunes.

Changing diapers isn't just for women anymore. We have better things to do with our time these days than rinse, wring, wash, dry, fold and stack.

Passing a law is one thing, but following it to the letter is quite another. I would suggest that each legislator, prior to voting, should hand-dip and rinse out one soiled diaper.

It's only a suggestion.

A Rural Love Story

It had all the elements of a real love story.

I began hearing about the star-crossed lovers, Alice and John, when we first moved to rural Minnesota over 20 years ago.

I was pretty naive at the time. It was my first experience with rural living and I had much to learn. After living in cities for all of my life, it was rather earth-shattering to discover that chickens don't need roosters in order to lay eggs and that not all meat is wrapped in cellophane.

I wanted to believe in the couple because their story was like a remake of "Romeo and Juliet."

We may not have had the feuding Montagues and Capulets, but we did have plenty of Olsons and Johnsons and they were fairly well divided in their loyalties to Alice or John.

"I'm a John Dear man," more than one farmer was heard to say. One of our neighbors in the country wore what he called the "John Dear colors", green and yellow.

Many other farmers pledged their undying loyalty to Alice Chalmers.

It soon became obvious that there were plenty of reasons why John and Alice didn't just run off and get married. The main reason was that neither of them could drive.

"I'm taking the Alice Chalmers into the shop," noted one of our neighbors. On other occasions, John Dear would be dropped off at the shop by another neighbor.

It was interesting to note that when people talked about John or Alice, their names were always prefaced with a "the". I figured that it was some reverent title, not unlike "his majesty" or "his honor."

Another reason for their failure to get married was depression, a malady shared by both John and Alice.

"The John Dear broke down in the middle of the cornfield," stated one concerned friend. Alice also had her share of breakdowns.

John and Alice had breakdowns in the most unlikely places: bean fields, in the middle of some farmyard or behind a barn. Their friends knew how to snap them out of their foul moods, however. They would take them to the shop again. Evidently, shopping always lifted their spirits.

A few weeks after I first heard about the couple and their divided camps of loyal supporters, I began reading the logos on feed caps. One read "John Deere." Another read "Allis Chalmers."

It was with some disappointment that I realized that John and Alice were figments of my imagination. I added two and two and came up with - farm machinery.

Rural living may be exciting at times but it's rarely a scene out of "Romeo and Juliet."

Walking on a Frozen Lake

I can't walk on water. Even if it's frozen.

My adventure on a frozen lake was a typical case of having a good idea but lacking the courage.

The idea was to write a newspaper feature story about an ice fisherman. I made arrangements to meet the angler near his favorite fishing hole on one cold Saturday. It would be an interesting story about a man who hated fish so much that he was willing to give up the warm comfort of his home and spend hours on a frozen lake. I had no idea that walking on the lake's surface could be such a harrowing experience.

The man assured me on the phone that his ice house was "just a piece" from the shore. In this case a piece was closer to a mile.

As I stood on the shore, where the ice met the sand, I could see dark specks, which later proved to be icehouses, cars, trucks and people, far out on the lake.

With my camera hanging from my neck and my notebook held in a tight grip, I stepped out onto the ice and faced my rendezvous with destiny.

The first twenty yards weren't all that menacing. The ice was a thick, creamy white and it felt solid beneath my feet. No problem. After all, if the lake could hold the weight of those vehicles and buildings, it could certainly hold up one more person.

I continued my steady shuffle, and without warning, the ice became crystal clear and it was possible to see where the ice left off and the water began. I began seeing cracks in the ice. Deep cracks, which reminded me of the yawning fizzures in the earthquake movies I had seen as a child.

If the ice had split there once before, what would keep it from happening again?

When I looked behind me, the shore appeared far off in the distance. In front of me, the specks seemed as remote as ever.

There was no wind and there were no sounds of civilization where I stood. As I continued to walk, one cautious step after another, I heard my first ping on the icy surface.

There was one ping and then another. I was positive I could hear the ice sigh and moan from all sides.

I recalled hearing about the dangers of dark ice on the radio one time. Compared to the ice cubes in my refrigerator, this was dark ice.

The halfway point between the shore and the buildings on the lake was finally reached. My feet and hands were numb with the cold and I wanted to go home. In all of my life, I had never felt so alone and helpless.

Unable to move, I stood still and listened to the ice making noises. For one fleeting second, I considered lying flat on the ice so I wouldn't fall through.

A voice deep inside me whispered, "The show must go on." That may be fine and dandy advice for someone on a dry theatre stage, but it simply doesn't cut it when you're looking death in the face on a cold, frozen lake.

I turned around and went home. Later, I called the fisherman and agreed to meet him at another time.

He's going to meet me on the shore.

When it comes to walking on ice, I simply have cold feet.

Musical Warfare

Fact can be stranger than fiction.

The U.S. Military has entered a new dimension: musical warfare. Actually, it's an offensive tactic that parents of teenagers have known about for many years.

After Manuel Antonio Noriega sought refuge in the Vatican Embassy in Panama before his surrender, loudspeakers were placed in the streets by the Americans, and the neighborhood reverberated with the nerve-racking strains of rap music.

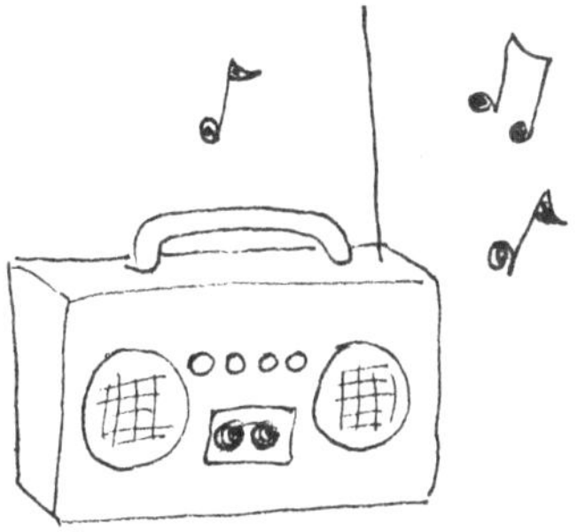

Theoretically, the music was intended to send Noriega, an opera fan, screaming into the streets and begging for silence. Consequently, he would be seized and arrested. As this column was being written, the latest news was that the rap music had been replaced with raucous rock and roll.

It won't work. For years, our own children tried to drive us out of the house with everything from Billy Joel to Bon Jovi, but we steadfastly refused to leave.

The musical approach to warfare opens up an entire new reign of military terror and ingenuity. As our armed forces convert their weapons from bayonets to Top Ten cassettes, CD's, woofers and tweeters, we enter a completely new arena of military strategies.

Banter at future summit meetings will include veiled threats: "We have a mural that will knock your socks off" and "We have enough sculptures to take over the world."

Eventually, world leaders will talk about stereo disarmament and the proliferation of rock stations.

If the musical tactics work in Panama, it is very likely that record and musical tape clubs will become the most powerful lobbyists in our nation's capitol.

A large percentage of the defense budget will include purchases of tape head cleaners and boom boxes. With the Pentagon typically buying cassette tapes at $1,500 each, stock investments in recording companies will skyrocket.

Politicians will be elected on the basis of their knowledge of ballet and watercolors. Rock singers will be named to the top Cabinet posts and Casey Kasem will become the Secretary of Sate.

It would be interesting to talk to the military advisor who dreamed up the idea of street loudspeakers in Panama. Undoubtedly, it was the parent of teenagers.

The Homecoming

Something strange happens to grown children when they return home for the holidays. They regress. They become children again and our world is turned upside down.

During the rest of the year, they are responsible adults in a dog-eat-dog world. They pay bills, carry on intelligent conversations, buy groceries and survive quite nicely. They are capable of sending in their own responses to magazine sweepstakes. They sort out the lights from the darks at the laundromat.

Quite inexplicably, all of their attempts to appear adult are cast off with their coats the moment they enter our front door.

Perhaps the way they act is a subconscious desire to make us feel young and needed once more. I hate to tell them this, but washing their bath towels four times a day and playing the role of short order cook just won't do it. If anything, I feel much older.

After observing them through Thanksgiving and Christmas, I wonder how they manage to cope in the outside world. They giggle, they laugh and they wrestle. Having them around is like living in a time warp.

The only difference between having the children around 20 years ago and having them around now is that we can no longer send them to their rooms.

When they're not around, our life is orderly. I have my favorite chair; my husband has his. We watch certain televison programs and we have our own places at the kitchen table. There are times when we talk and there are times when we don't.

Total chaos breaks out when the girls return home.

My favorite chair is no longer mine. I can't crawl

into bed without hurdling over a dozen opened suitcases.

Without a reservation system in effect, the bathroom becomes inaccessible. I can't recall brushing my teeth without at least two other people sharing the same room.

Then they left. Extra leaves were removed from the tables and the Christmas decorations were packed away for another year. Extra bedrooms were closed off and I regained possession of my favorite chair in the living room.

The house is quiet now. Too quiet.

Having my own chair isn't all that great.

The Foraging Festival

The Foraging Festival has come to an end.

For over a month, between Thanksgiving and New Year's Day, we have done our best to eliminate every piece of peanut brittle, every candy cane and every cup of egg nog. We grazed from room to room, food tray to food tray, devouring every morsel of food in sight.

We are not alone.

According to a magazine article I read this week, an estimated 34 million Americans are overweight and still expanding. It's somehow reassuring to know we have company.

Americans appear to be divided into two basic groups: eaters and maladjusted non-eaters. Half of us pursue the subliminal promises of immortality with physical fitness programs and by eating vast amounts of yogurt and lettuce. The other half is selflessly doing its best to maintain the gross national product.

Granted, the physical fitness craze has resulted in a $25 billion industry. Although I don't have the exact figures, I would guess that the junk food industry is pulling in the same amount on any given day.

Eaters serve a noble purpose. For example, if it weren't for us 34 billion eaters, with whom would the non-eaters compare themselves?

Without eaters, the economic growth of the country would falter miserably.

If all women in this country wore size three, the textile mills of the South would also shrink in size because less fabric would be needed for clothing. Somewhere there's a cotton field with my name on it.

The same economic slump would extend to bakeries, chocolate shops and potato chip factories.

The economic health of our nation would be devastated. A country can only manufacture so many exercise machines and bathroom scales.

With everyone eating tossed salads and other foods good for them, even the antacid industry would go stomach-up.

Fast food restaurants would no longer exist and golden arches would become artifacts of the past. A wing of the Smithsonian would have to be dedicated to the distant memories of potato chips dips and hot fudge sundaes.

We shouldn't feel guilty about eating. If anything, we should be thanked.

To paraphrase poet John Milton, "They also serve, who only sit and eat."

Long-Distance Parenting

While we all lived under the same roof, it seemed much easier to solve our daughters' problems.

If a doll's leg fell off, or a math problem was too difficult or a car ran out of gas, my husband and I would quickly react. Armed with a well-worn book by Dr. Spock, assorted sizes of bandages and sound advice passed down through generations, there were few problems we couldn't solve. As parents, we were invincible.

Since the girls moved off to college, we have discovered that being a long-distance repairman is next to impossible.

Our oldest daughter called home this week with news that her car wouldn't start. Her father's immediate reaction was to jump into the car and go to her rescue like any good caped crusader.

The main obstacle to his heroic efforts was the fact she lives in Chicago, a good ten-hour drive away. Outside of reciting some worn-out homilies like "Everything will be all right" and "This too shall pass", there was little he could do. Sending jumper cables to her by way of Western Union seemed out of the question.

Somewhere along the way, we lost control in solving their problems. Once they move away, it's hard to kiss where it hurts and come off sounding like Dr. Ruth.

We are no longer dispensers of sage advice, but rather we have assumed the roles of sounding boards for all of the world's ills, with no response required, thank you.

One evening, the same daughter called with the message that unless the master computer for her campus would be repaired overnight and a bookkeeping error would be unraveled, she would not be able to register for her second semester. For all practical purposes, her world had come to an end.

I tossed and turned all night as I thought about college computer systems gone amuck and my daughter's future hanging by a slim thread of hope.

She never called back.

About a week later, I called to ask her how her registration had gone.

"Fine," she responded. "It wasn't a big deal."

Last school year, another daughter called us every time a fire was set in her dormitory. There were many sleepless nights as I envisioned her standing out in a snow bank in her bare feet while her dormitory burned to the ground.

Being a long-distance parent requires a good, strong heart. It took several years for us to realize that they only call when a problem rears its ugly head. If we don't hear from them, everything is fine.

We are now taking a new approach to parenting. If they call to tell us that their campuses have burned to the ground and all of their professors have fled to Buenos Aires to become circus clowns, we will not panic. Everything will be cleared up by the next morning.

My Husband's Past Life

It was like opening a time capsule.

My husband discovered the undeveloped roll of 127 film while he was cleaning out some old boxes in the basement.

There are probably similar boxes in other homes. Transferred from one house to another, from one city to another, from basement to garage to attic, there are a certain number of boxes, simply labeled "miscellaneous." They hold old Boy Scout uniforms, high school term papers and faded snapshots showing people long-forgotten.

The roll of film was a complete mystery. It was also a challenge. Discovering the film was one thing -finding someone to develop it was another. A local photo studio finally agreed to send off the film with no promises attached.

It had been at least 25 years since we had used 127 film in our cameras. Would the photos show us as a younger couple, without children and gray hair? It was difficult to imagine that images suspended in time on film would last very long.

The call finally came one afternoon this week. The photos were in.

At the studio, I hurriedly wrote a check for the processing and tore open the envelope containing the mystery photos.

One photo showed my mother-in-law wearing glasses I had never seen before and darker hair.

Another photo showed her husband's head, complete with an unfamiliar brushcut. There were a couple of blurred photos and one of what appeared to be an interstate highway intersection.

The last two photos were the most startling. One showed four smiling cheerleaders, vintage 1950s. The second showed the twirling skirts of, supposedly, the same cheerleaders.

Using a keen sense of deduction which I had picked up from Nancy Drew novels, I figured out that the photos had been taken by my husband at least 30 years ago, before we met.

It was especially disconcerting that I had paid several dollars to have photos of strange cheerleaders developed. In all of the time I have known him, my husband has never demonstrated an active interest in cheerleaders or swirling cheerleader skirts.

To further complicate matters, when I confronted my husband with the misadventures of his past, he feigned complete innocence.

No experience in life is without its lessons. Judging from this adventure, I have learned that the expiration date on film isn't necessarily carved in stone. Who knows? Perhaps some film used this year could be developed in the year 2020.

I will also watch my husband much more closely when the Dallas Cheerleaders appear on television.

The Cabbage Problem

Consider for a moment the most recent plight of the Chinese. If you're a gardener, you will certainly identify with their cabbage dilemma.

After ordering peasants in Beijing's suburbs to grow more cabbage this year, Chinese officials also created incentives by raising cabbage prices.

In previous years the residents of Beijing had been limited to 66 pounds of cabbage per person. Because of the unexpected cabbage glut on the market, each person is now being coerced into buying 110 pounds of cabbage.

That's a lot of cole slaw.

One worker noted that he and his wife had to buy 110 pounds of cabbage apiece. In light of the fact that the perishable vegetable would have to be stored in their apartment, they were giving serious thought to moving out to make room for the long-stemmed Chinese cabbage.

The cabbage situation in Beijing brought back not so fond memories of the summer I grew zucchini squash. Our family ate so much zucchini that summer that our skin began turning green.

Sympathetic friends shared their recipes for zucchini bread, zucchini bars and zucchini cookies. In return for their thoughtfulness, I gave them squash. The situation finally got to the point when my friends began avoiding me out of fear they would receive another car trunkful of zucchini.

The squash were much like gray hairs - as soon as I would pluck one from the garden, three more would take its place.

I tried frying, breading and baking zucchini, but it was a losing battle. The plants proved to be more prolific than rabbits and for the first time in my life, I prayed for a killing frost.

As the vines spread out of the garden and ran rampant over the lawn, our yard resembled an Amazonian rain forest. Runaway vines would clutch at our legs if we ventured too close to the garden. We could only imagine what was lurking beneath the undergrowth.

Although I have lived through avalanches of giant tomatoes and mountains of cucumbers, nothing compared with the summer of the insidious zucchini squash.

It's hard to imagine eating 110 pounds of cabbage. Hopefully, the Beijing officials are also handing out recipes for cabbage cake and cabbage cookies.

The Turkey

I always seem to have trouble choosing turkeys and Christmas trees, and this year is no exception.

We have never had a small, compact Christmas tree. They never sit neatly and unobtrusively in a corner. Once their branches have adjusted to indoor temperatures, our trees take over the entire living room. There are few movie scenes which would rival the horror of seeing a Christmas tree as it takes over a three-bedroom house.

As soon as its branches are decorated and it has been allowed to settle, it is possible for a five-foot spruce to resemble a national forest. Left on its own, it is capable of obstructing all traffic in the house and tripping unsuspecting guests.

My main problem seems to be that, when I buy a tree, there is no such thing as too big.

Our Thanksgiving turkey this year was so big that it had to start thawing out soon after Labor Day. It was the king of all turkeys.

The turkey was gargantuan to begin with, and once it was thawed out and stuffed, it appeared to double in size. I had so much trouble wedging it into the oven that I seriously considered using a crowbar.

It continued to grow in the oven. By the time dinner was served, the turkey dwarfed the other dishes on the dining room table. In fact, it dwarfed everything in sight. I actually felt skinny standing next to the monstrous bird.

We tried our best to eat our way through the mountain of turkey. Our guests were encouraged to attend an instant replay of the dinner four hours later and there still was a ton of turkey left after the second assault.

As I faced the challenge of turkey leftovers, I

tried every trick in the cookbook. Since Thanksgiving we have had turkey salads, turkey casseroles and turkey sandwiches. We have eaten so much turkey that we may soon begin to sprout feathers.

This chapter of our lives could justifiably be called The Revenge of the Turkey. The leftovers have taken over my life. I have camouflaged so much turkey meat that it's anyone's guess which will leave me first, my family or the leftovers.

The good news is that the end is in sight. One good sized meal of creamed turkey should finish off the leftovers.

I do know one thing for sure. We won't have turkey for Christmas dinner this year. Perhaps I'll buy ham this time. Not too big, but maybe large enough for a dinner and a few leftovers. After all, a ham can never be too big.

Briny Burials

The latest pollution concern in England isn't plastic bags, landfills or car exhausts. It's the growing demand for burials at sea.

Briny burials have doubled over the past five years, and although special permits are issued by the Agriculture Ministry, illegal burials are also increasing. As a result, too many bodies, in various states of disrepair, are littering the bottom of the sea.

It's not a pretty picture.

Because of England's historical ties to the sea, ocean burials have always been popular. After reading countless novels by Joseph Conrad and Herman Melville, I can understand the Britons' fascination with watery wakes.

Every good ocean adventure worth its salt has at least one emotion-filled scene when a body is wrapped in a white sheet and is slipped into the sea.

The captain, who invariably bears a strong resemblance to Gregory Peck or Jimmy Stewart, intones, "Into the sea we commend the soul of our dearly departed."

Tears flow from the eyes of even the crustiest sailors, and some unseen orchestra plays in the background. There's a single splash and the plot moves onto the next scene, either involving a stowaway or a full-fledged mutiny.

The main problem with the practice today is that biodegradable Englishmen are receiving their final rinse in non-biodegradable caskets. This poses a great dilemma for commercial fishermen who apparently dislike surprises.

It's easy to understand their reluctance to cast out nets for tuna or mackerel and come up with someone's aunt. If nothing else, it would certainly take the fun out of fishing.

The new customs can't be helping the sheet industry, either.

In spite of the pollution concerns, I'm still intrigued with the notion of being buried at sea. It sounds much more romantic than being planted in the third lot, 22nd row of some piece of real estate going by the name of "Sunnyside Acres" or "Peaceful Gardens".

In the worst case scenario, it wouldn't be all that bad to have a shipful of browny, handsome fishermen refer to me as "the one that got away."

Additional copies of POTATO CHIPS ARE VEGETABLES or NEVER TRUST A SIZE THREE may be ordered from:

BARE BONES BOOKS
315 NORTH FREEMAN
LUVERNE, MN 56156

This order form may be photocopied. Wholesale orders may be placed through Prairie House, Inc., Suite F, 1335 Second Avenue North, Fargo, ND 58102.

Please send me ________ copies of POTATO CHIPS ARE VEGETABLES and/or ________ copies of NEVER TRUST A SIZE THREE at $9.95 each. (An additional $2 is required for 1-4 books for postage and handling.)

Enclosed is my check or money order for $______ payable to BARE BONES BOOKS.

NAME ________________________________

STREET ______________________________

CITY________________STATE______ZIP______